BC
SHi
RE/
WR
THF

FIN
INC
BF

The Alaska Handbook

The Alaska Handbook

by
R. K. Woerner

McFarland & Company Inc., Publishers
Jefferson, North Carolina, and London

Library of Congress Cataloguing-in-Publication Data

Woerner, R. K.
The Alaska handbook.

Includes index.
1. Alaska—Handbooks, manuals, etc.
2. Alaska—Statistics.
I. Title.
F904.W7 1986   979.8'05   85-43599

ISBN 0-89950-219-9 (acid-free natural paper)

Printed in the United States of America

McFarland   Box 611   Jefferson NC 28640

Respectfully dedicated to the people of Alaska.

Acknowledgments

I wish to express my personal thanks to the U.S. Forest Service, the U.S. Department of the Interior National Parks Service, the Alaska Department of Fish and Game for their sportfishing predictions, the Federal Aviation Administration, the State of Alaska Department of Tourism, and the Alaskan Chambers of Commerce. I also wish to thank the people of Alaska for their willing help in obtaining needed information. I particularly wish to thank Roy Middleton, a thirty-year resident of Alaska, for his assistance with the manuscript.

Contents

ARCTIC OCEAN

Barrow

Prudhoe
Bay

NORTH SLOPE

ARCTIC CIRCLE

CHUKCHI
SEA

BROOKS RANGE

U.S.S.R.

Kotzebue

ARCTIC CIRCLE

Livengood

ST. LAWRENCE
ISLAND

Nome

YUKON RIVER

Manley
Hot
Springs

Kaiyuh Mts

Fairbanks

YUKON DELTA

Kuskokwim Mountains

BERING
SEA

Palmer

Bethel

KIOKLUK MTS.

Anchorage

NUNIVAK
ISLAND

Kenai

Dillingham

Homer

Seward

PRIBILOF
ISLANDS

Kodiak

ALASKA PENINSULA

ALEUTIAN
ISLANDS

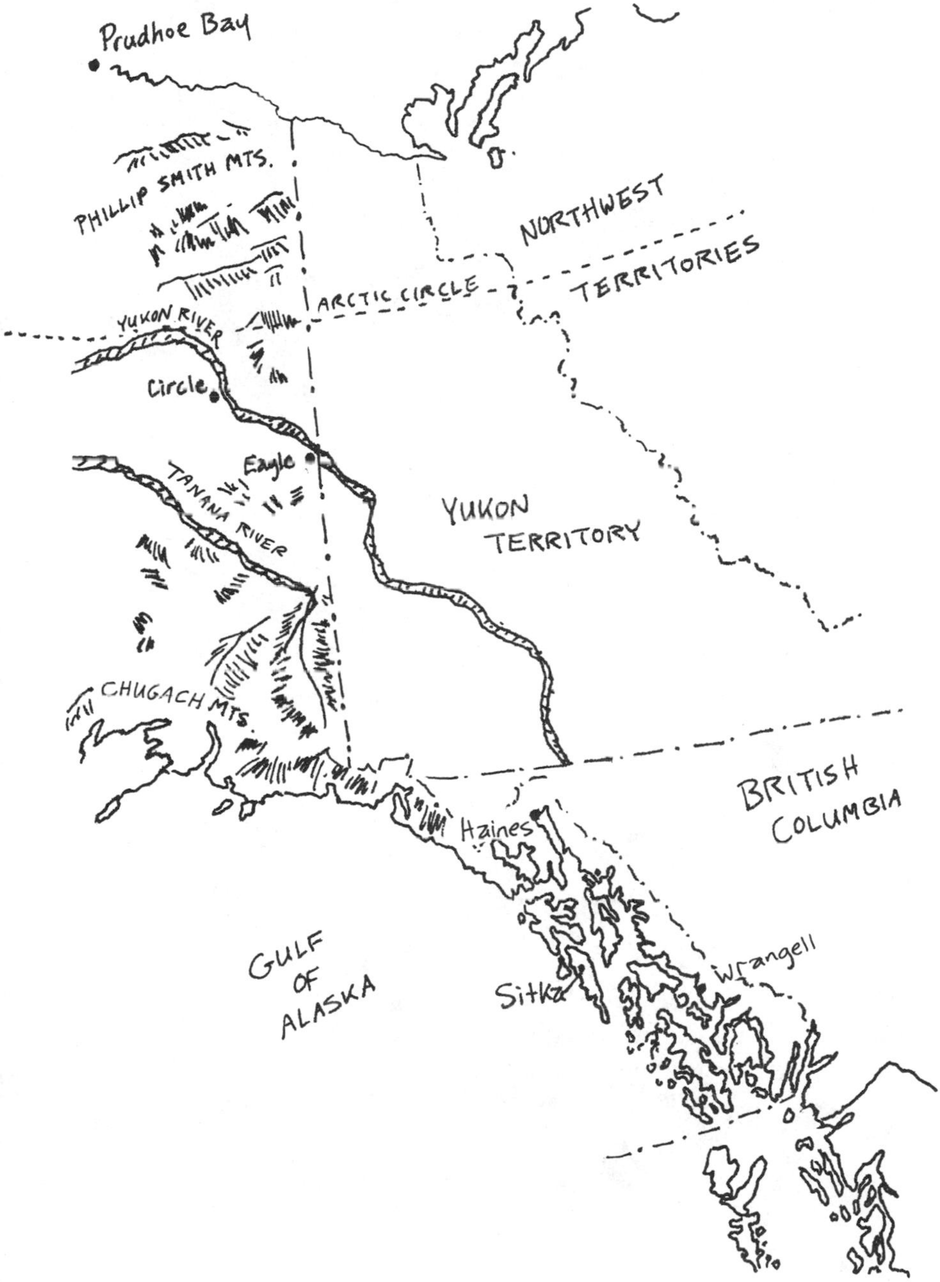

Prudhoe Bay

PHILLIP SMITH MTS.

NORTHWEST

TERRITORIES

ARCTIC CIRCLE

YUKON RIVER

Circle

Eagle

TANANA RIVER

YUKON
TERRITORY

CHUGACH MTS.

Haines

BRITISH
COLUMBIA

GULF
OF
ALASKA

Sitka

Wrangell

ALASKA

Area: 586,400 square miles
Population: 516,324
State capital: Juneau
State bird: Willow Ptarmigan
State fish: King Salmon
State flower: Forget-Me-Not
State gem: Jade
State mineral: Gold
State tree: Sitka Spruce

1. Alaska: An Overview

The state of Alaska, the largest state in the United States and the forty-ninth to be admitted to the Union, has developed a reputation as America's last great frontier, a reputation well deserved if you consider Alaska's physical geography. A mighty peninsula surrounded by two oceans and two seas, Alaska is still largely a virgin wilderness filled with majestic mountain ranges, vast forests and countless rivers, some of them still unnamed. There are places in this state where a man can go and not be seen for months, if that is what he wishes. Alaska's lure is varied and seemingly endless. It runs the gamut from glaciers, ice and snow, to smoking volcanoes, desert sand, grassy tundra and rain forests. Alaska is a land of untold wealth and indescribable beauty, a land where great herds of caribou still roam and Dall sheep play on precarious mountain ledges. It is a place where the sounds of the wings of thousands of birds can still at times be heard overhead, and where the noise of thousands of sea lions can overpower the crash of the surf on the beaches. Alaska is a place where brilliant fields of fireweed can be seen on summer days, and where tiny tundra flowers rejoice at the coming of spring.

Vast untapped mineral resources in Alaska are now in the process of being located and developed, and perhaps because of this, Alaska is also a land in a state of turmoil and conflict. The oil companies have moved in with their big money and machinery and are rapidly changing the state and its people. Battles are being waged by local and national organizations who are concerned, not only with Alaska's welfare, but with their own as well. Federal interference, ecological battles, native rights, exploitation, and even foreign fishermen are a few of the worries with which the state must contend at the present time. Alaska is now in a position unique among states, that of deciding and shaping the course of her future, something that happened years ago in the lower forty-eight and was decided, for good or for ill, by generations past. How Alaska resolves these issues and the decisions that she makes now will determine the kind of life that future generations of Alaskans will live. In this sense also Alaska is a last frontier, and its people could be called true modern-day pioneers.

1

Size and Population

The word Alaska comes from the Aleut term *alyeska*, which means "the great land," and Alaska's proportions certainly fit that description. The state contains 586,400 square miles, more than twice the area of Texas. It is 2400 miles from east to west and 1420 miles from north to south. Alaska's coastline is 33,904 miles long, greater than all of the other coastal states combined. Yet, in spite of the state's large size, Alaska's permanent population was estimated to be only 516,324 people in February of 1984—fewer than live in the city of Atlanta, Georgia. Many of the people who make up the latest population figures have moved there in the recent past. The 1980 census showed a population figure of 407,500. In 1982, the population had grown to 460,837. The National Planning Association, a private firm that studies the national economy and makes economic forecasts, predicts that by the year 2000, Alaska's population will have increased by fifty percent over 1980 figures. The rate of growth will be 2.1 percent per year, compared to the national average of .8 percent, a rate that makes it the fastest growing state in the United States.

One reason for the growth is that people are finding out that the old notion of Alaska as a barren wilderness with one perpetual season of ice and snow is simply not true. Granted, there is a long, dark winter with almost unbelievably cold temperatures in some places, but there is also a delightfully mild summer and an elusive but strikingly beautiful fall and spring. The state is not all wilderness either; there are busy modern cities and friendly towns and villages with efficient transportation systems and modern hotels and department stores. For the visitor to Alaska, nearly everything is possible, from the solitude of the complete wilderness experience to the finest accommodations civilization has to offer anywhere.

Geology

Geologically speaking, Alaska is a young land when compared to other areas of the United States. Volcanoes, glaciers, earthquakes, and giant tidal waves are still shaping the face of the land.

As recently as June 6, 1912, one of the volcanoes on the Alaska Peninsula, Mt. Novarupta, suddenly turned a peaceful mountain valley into a raging inferno. The volcano exploded, sending forth masses of pumice and rock fragments and 2½ cubic miles of white-hot ash. Six miles to the east, the molten lava core of Mt. Katmai drained into the earth and was promptly expelled by Novarupta, causing the entire top of Mt. Katmai to collapse. Magma filled the steaming valleys to depths as great as 700 feet.

Earthquakes shook the land for three days, and cities close to the eruption were buried in ash.

The notorious Good Friday earthquake of March 27, 1964 — the most severe earthquake ever recorded on the North American Continent — occurred in southcentral Alaska. In the space of a few moments, 50,000 square miles of land heaved, dropped, or slipped with a force measuring 8.4 on the Richter scale. The face of much of Alaska was permanently altered in those moments. Landslides dammed rivers and swept away roads and railroads; huge areas of earth slid into the sea; land suddenly rose many feet in some areas, leaving deep-water piers high and dry. In other areas, land rapidly sank, drowning whole forests of spruce. Seismic waves added to the devastation of many communities already severely damaged by the quake. Valdez was almost completely destroyed by the giant waves, and Kodiak, far to the south in the Gulf of Alaska, also suffered extensive damage. The aftermath of the quake can still be seen in Anchorage's Earthquake Park, located on the bluffs above Cook Inlet, where homes in a residential subdivision were torn apart as sections of the bluff gave way and sank to the level of the beach below.

Tidal waves are also fairly common in Alaska. In fact, the Cook Inlet area ranks ninth in the world in frequency of tidal waves. On at least five different occasions in recent history, giant tidal waves here swept into Lituya Bay near Yakutat on the Gulf of Alaska, the most recent in 1958. On that occasion an earthquake sent ninety million tons of rock and earth hurtling into the bay, throwing up a wave 1,720 feet high, which scoured the hills to bedrock. The tree line that records the high-water mark left by this great wave can still be seen in Lituya Bay.

Glaciers and rivers are also very active in shaping the face of the state. The glaciers are busy carving great valleys and grinding mountain slopes, while some of the rivers deposit gravel and sedimentation so fast that channels change quickly and bars and islands are formed practically overnight. One of the most dramatic demonstrations of the erosive action of water can be found in Alaska's historic "self-dumping" lakes. One such was Lake George, in the Chugach Mountain Range of southcentral Alaska. Each winter the Knik Glacier would slowly advance until it met the unyielding face of the granite cliff of the Knik River Valley, forming a plug behind which the waters of sixteen-mile-long Lake George would rapidly rise. Then, as the long days of summer warmed the lake waters and the face of the ice barrier, melting of ice at the foot of the glacier would begin. By August, with water at its highest and the glacier at its weakest, the ice dam would fall victim to its own mass and collapse, tearing itself into massive slabs, some as wide as 600 feet. In a matter of hours, the entire lake would empty into the valley. House-sized chunks of ice were hurtled downstream at express-train speeds, gouging giant boulders from the

Portage Glacier is one of the highway-accessible glaciers in Alaska. A visitor center and paved parking area provide lakeside convenience for viewing and photographing the glacier and the blue-white icebergs floating in Portage Lake at the Glacier's base.

walls of the valley, to rumble with the torrent toward distant Cook Inlet. As the raging waters poured down the valley, geysers of spray would shoot high into the air. Miles downstream, motorists crossing the Knik River bridge would note a dramatic rise in the river and the presence of blocks of drifting glacial ice, which signified that Lake George was once again a placid mountain stream. Land rearrangement caused by the 1964 earthquake brought an end to the self-dumping action of Lake George, but there are other such lakes that can still be found in Alaska.

Alaska's Natives

At the end of the ice age, when much of the world's oceans were still locked in ice, the water level was much lower than it is now. Many believe that the thousand-mile-wide continental shelf connecting Alaska and Siberia was then dry land. It was during this age that Alaska began to be populated as nomadic peoples filtered eastward over a period of thousands of years. Then, about 11,000 years ago, the earth's seas once again began to rise as the climate warmed, and the land bridge was finally covered with water. By this time, however, the hardy forebears of today's native Alaskans had managed to learn the arts of survival.

There are three separate groups of aboriginal peoples who make up Alaska's natives. Those sometimes known as "Eskimos" (a term no longer preferred) were once a nomadic people scattered across much of Alaska as far south as Prince William Sound. They comprise two main groups with two distinct languages: the Inupiaq and the Yup'ik. Except for those who have moved to the larger cities, these native Alaskans have now settled in villages which dot western and northern Alaska. They are a people of medium stature, noted for their strength and endurance, their love of poetry, music, and dance, and their excellent artists. Today the members of this native population living in Alaska number about 34,000.

In southwestern Alaska, along the fog-shrouded length of the Aleutian Island chain, another group of aboriginal Alaskans was found by early explorers. The origins of the Aleuts are something of a mystery. A seafaring people who are excellent navigators, the Aleuts have physical characteristics different from those of either Inuit or Indians. There are some similarities between the Aleuts and the Ainu peoples who inhabit the northern islands of Japan, so there is the possibility that early Aleuts could have arrived from the Orient; the distance would not have been too great for men who are known to be outstanding sailors. The Aleuts are usually taller than the Inuit, with lighter skin. They have always excelled at hunting and fishing, and still man many of the fishing boats which contribute so much to Alaska's economy. There are now 8,000 Aleuts living in Alaska.

Three major tribes make up the Alaskan community of Indians. The Athabascan, whose original territory covered most of interior Alaska, are members of North America's largest linguistic family. The Tlingit tribe occupied southeastern Alaska and some coastal areas of southwestern Alaska, while the Haida tribe was largely confined to the beautiful island of Prince of Wales in southeastern Alaska. Alaska's Indians were outstanding sailors, fishermen, and hunters and ranged throughout western waters in their large dugout canoes. By the time the first white men arrived in Alaska, the Indians had developed complex social and political systems. They were fierce fighters and in fact drove out the first Russians who tried to settle the town of Sitka.

The Alaskan Indians were skilled carvers, and their totems are still to be found in many areas throughout the state. Early missionaries burned many totems in the mistaken belief that they represented idols, but their real purpose was to record the history of the tribe and family. These carved cedar trees, sometimes as high as fifty feet, represented the history, family line, legend of some great event, and status of the carver.

The major groups of Alaskan Indians, and their numerous offshoots now add up to 22,000 people.

History

The Eskimos, the Aleuts, and a few small tribes of Indians comprised the total native population of Alaska until the early 1700s, when the Siberian Russians first explored the "great land" to the east. In 1725 Captain Vitus Bering, a Dane serving in the Russian navy, was commissioned by Peter the Great to seek new lands for Russia. Although he sailed through the strait which now bears his name in the year 1728, he did not actually see the North American lands because of unusually heavy fog. It wasn't until his second voyage in 1741 that he sighted the St. Elias Range in southeastern Alaska. His crew put ashore near Prince William Sound on St. Elias Island, now called Kayak Island, and became the first white men to set foot on Alaskan soil.

Bering's crew returned to Russia with an abundance of rich furs. Russian traders, seeing this new land as a promising source of furs, began pushing the czar to take possession of the land. In 1783 the first permanent Russian settlement was established on Kodiak Island. During the next fifty years other Russian settlements were established throughout coastal Alaska. The most notable of these settlements was Sitka.

Other nations also noticed Alaska during this period. For example, England's Captain James Cook discovered Cook Inlet in 1778 and also explored the coastline, naming many landmarks. English traders from Hudson's Bay Company moved overland from Canada in the same year as Cook and set up a trading post at Fort Yukon on the Yukon River. Bodega Quadra, who sailed north from California, explored the area around Sitka for Spain. Americans were the last to come, but once they realized the tremendous potential in fur trading and whaling, they flocked to Alaska in great numbers.

Alexander Baranof was sent to Alaska by the Russian czar in 1791 to reorganize the Russian American Company and to obtain a fur trade charter, which he did in 1799. Baranof ruled Alaska as a self-appointed czar. He enslaved the natives into working for his company and built schools, churches, sawmills, tanneries, and foundries. In a violent reaction to Baranof's mistreatment, the Tlingit Indians massacred a large number of Russians at Sitka and destroyed the town. In 1802, Baranof rebuilt the town of Sitka; in 1806, he moved the capital from Kodiak to Sitka. Sitka became a boomtown during Baranof's time, drawing adventurers and explorers from all parts of the world, and was often called "the Paris of the Pacific."

When Alexander Baranof died in 1819, the city seemed to die with him. Following Baranof's death, the Russians attempted to close the southeastern Alaska coastline to British and American traders. However, unable to enforce their closed-coast policy and under constant pressure from American fur traders, the Russians granted equal trading rights to the Americans in 1824, and to the British in 1825.

By the 1850s, competition made trade in Alaska very unprofitable for Russia. War with the English in the Crimea convinced the Russians that their Alaska holdings were barely tenable at best. So it was that in 1867, Baron Edouard de Stoekl, the Russian minister to the United States, proposed selling Alaska to the United States. Secretary of State William H. Seward signed a treaty of Cession of Russian America to the United States on March 30, 1867, and persuaded Congress to approve the purchase for $7,200,000, or about two cents per acre. The American flag was raised over Alaskan soil at Sitka on October 18, 1867. At that time there were only 483 whites in Alaska, and only 150 of these were actually United States citizens. The purchase was called "Seward's Folly" by those who opposed it, and Alaska soon acquired the nickname of "Seward's Ice Box."

For the next two decades, Alaska suffered shameful neglect at the hands of its distant government. Administration was assigned to the Treasury Department, and for years the only federal officials in the territory were customs agents and the army. In 1877, the army was withdrawn, and sole authority to govern the 40,000 people now living in the territory was given to the customs collector at Sitka. Two years later, fearing an Indian uprising, the residents of Sitka were forced to call on the British navy to send a warship to provide protection.

In spite of these and other problems, American expansion continued. Since the days of earliest exploration, it was known that gold could be found in Alaska, and small gold rushes had occurred at Wrangell, Alaska, and in the Cassiar in neighboring British Columbia. In 1881, two prospectors discovered a mountain of low-grade gold ore at Juneau, which developed into the Juneau and Treadwell mines. For many years these mines were among the richest in the world, processing over 250,000 tons of ore per year.

Then on June 17, 1897, the steamer *Portland* tied up in Seattle with a shipment of $800,000 in gold dust from a fabulous new strike on the Klondike River in Canada's Yukon Territory, just across the boundary from Alaska. Almost immediately one of history's biggest gold rushes was on. During the next two years an estimated quarter of a million people started north for the diggings, and some 50,000 actually made it, many suffering incredible hardships along the way. Most arrived at Skagway by way of steamer and then hiked the passes to Dawson in the Yukon. By November of 1897, 3,700 horses lay dead in White Pass, and the shorter but steeper Chilkoot Pass was described as looking like a battlefield. Lawlessness ran rampant, and it was said that in Skagway there was a killing a day.

In 1898, gold was also discovered at Cape Nome on the Seward Peninsula, and by 1899, some 3,000 miners were panning streams in that area.

Top: *The Holy Assumption Church in Kenai. The oldest Russian Orthodox church in Alaska, it contains a 200-year-old Bible and is still in use today.* Bottom: *Across the street, the St. Nicholas Chapel marks the burial place of Father Egumen Nicolai, who founded Holy Assumption in 1846.*

By August of 1900, gold had also been found on Nome's black sand beaches; 232 ships and an additional 18,000 people arrived soon afterward. Unlike Skagway, Nome quickly adopted a criminal and civil code and formed a judicial system that curbed lawlessness and brought strong order to that region.

The gold strikes were rich ones indeed. In the Klondike alone, a 30×40 mile area, over one billion dollars in gold had been removed by 1904.

There's gold in them thar hills! To the surprise and delight of these teenagers, a rest stop at a creek along the highway yields tiny flecks of gold, quickly cached in a handy sandwich bag. Recreational gold panning is a popular activity in many parts of Alaska, and many lodges offer this as one of their scheduled activities.

It was not until 1912 that Alaska was granted true territorial status, with her own legislature. For forty-five years she had no governing body but Congress. For thirty-nine years she had no representation in Congress. When territorial status was finally granted, Alaska's population had grown until it was denser than any other territory had claimed when granted territorial rights, with the exception of Montana.

Great amounts of land were set aside for federal use during Theodore Roosevelt's administration. In fact, most of Alaska today is still made up of federally owned lands.

Construction of the Alaska Railroad from Seward to Fairbanks began in 1914. Major construction camps were set up at Ship Creek on Cook Inlet, which later became the city of Anchorage.

In 1935, during the Great Depression, a farm colonization effort was initiated when the government transported two hundred destitute families from Minnesota, Michigan and Wisconsin to the famed Matanuska Valley near Anchorage. Many of the descendants of these original families still operate farms near Palmer, about forty miles northeast of Anchorage.

Alaska's value as a strategic defense post for the rest of the nation became blatantly apparent during World War II. When Japan declared war on America in 1941, a road from the United States through Canada to Alaska became an immediate necessity. In 1942, thousands of men poured into Canada and Alaska. In an unbelievable eight months, they had constructed the Alaska Highway over the entire 1523-mile route from Dawson Creek to Fairbanks. By 1943, more than 140,000 military personnel were stationed in Alaska. In that same year, one of the bloodiest battles of World War II was fought at Attu in the Aleutian Islands. Many of the men stationed in Alaska returned at the war's end to settle there permanently.

From Alaska's earliest days as a territory, many residents had favored the idea of statehood. Since her purchase, Alaska had contributed far more than any other territory to the nation's treasury. Unlike other territories in the continental United States, Alaska stood alone as the territory with a foreign nation lying between herself and the rest of the country; yet most Americans gave little thought to their northern outpost until pressures for statehood both within and without the state forced the issue. Finally, on June 30, 1958, Congress passed the Alaska Statehood Bill, which was approved and ratified by President Dwight D. Eisenhower. On August 25th of that same year, Alaskans voted in a special election to accept statehood. The president proclaimed Alaska a state on January 3, 1959.

Oil and the Economy

On March 13, 1968, on the barren north slope of Alaska's Arctic, an oil company drilling bit broke through the barrier of rock and earth into a strata of oil-bearing sand described as one of the richest ever found. This discovery was the culmination of forty years of exploration on the slope and more than a half century of oil development within Alaska. Some think it also marked the turning point in the "boom and bust" cycles that have dominated Alaska's economy since territorial days, namely the rushes for furs, fish, and gold and the military spending spree during World War II – all of which ended abruptly and left Alaska to weather the "bust" that inevitably followed.

The Prudhoe Oil Strike was definitely the beginning of a new boom. The lease sale of state land for oil exploration purposes on September 10, 1969, netted the state over 900 million dollars in bonus monies alone. After oil began flowing through the pipeline in June of 1977, the state began collecting taxes and royalties, which in 1978 accounted for fifty-five percent of all state revenue. The percentage rose to sixty-nine percent in 1979, eighty-six percent in 1980, and has remained at about that level up to the present time.

The National Petroleum Council has estimated that half the nation's undiscovered oil and gas reserves are in Alaska, and exploration continues. Arco is already well along with development of the Kuparuk field, which they believe contains about 1.2 billion barrels of oil. The Shell Oil Company has announced a new oil discovery on manmade Seal Island in the Beaufort Sea. Initial yields of high-grade crude are from 600 to 5000 barrels a day. If the well proves to be of commercial value, the state could receive ninety-one percent of net profits from the well because of the "percent of net profits" bidding system under which the land was leased to the oil company. The boom is on – but this time the sustained sharp decline which traditionally follows is not expected to recur in the process of developing the state's petroleum reserves. The revenues generated from petroleum development are expected to provide a strong, continuing base for the Alaskan economy.

In the last twenty-five years, Alaskans have laid the groundwork for a modern economy; they now have the opportunity to build on it. While oil revenues are expected to continue and can broaden the economic base, that base is presently very narrow. Only about thirteen percent of Alaska's workforce is directly employed by the industries that are Alaska's backbone. The 27,000 workers (44,000 extra in the summer) who work in oil, mining, fishing, and lumbering are the only ones who tap the natural resources that indirectly support the rest of Alaska's workforce. From such a narrow base, the rest of the workforce sort of blossoms out like a bush, ending up rather wide and topheavy. Government is by far the biggest employer and, next to oil, generates the most revenue for the state. Tourism runs a close second in the number of people employed, and is third in the amount of revenue generated. Nearly 700,000 people visited Alaska in 1983, spending nearly $500 million while they were there. Retail and service industries employ most of the other workers.

In 1976 Alaska wisely established, by voter-approved constitutional

amendment, the Alaska Permanent Fund, a sort of trust fund for the Alaskan people that receives a minimum of twenty-five percent each year of nontax resource revenues. The monies in the permanent fund may not be used directly for state operating expenses, but interest income from the permanent fund is allowed to go into the state's general fund. Permanent fund monies are used to make income-producing investments. The idea behind the permanent fund is to stash away the money now while it is plentiful to provide a continuous source of revenue against the time when nonrenewable resources such as oil have been exhausted.

In 1982 a state permanent fund dividend program was established by which dividend payments are distributed to Alaskan citizens of six months or longer. The payments are determined by dividing half of the permanent fund earnings by the number of applicants for dividend checks. In 1982 every man, woman, and child over the age of six months who applied received a dividend check of $1000.00. In 1983 the dividend check amounted to $386.15. There is now roughly $5.5 billion in the Alaska Permanent Fund; that amount is expected to grow to $17 billion by the year 2000.

The remaining seventy-five percent of nontax revenues (there is no state income tax in Alaska) and other revenue generated by the permanent fund is being used in various ways to improve the quality of life. It is being used to improve educational facilities, particularly in the more remote regions of the state. It is being used to construct hydroelectric projects in several areas of the southeastern portion, and on the Susitna River in southcentral Alaska. It is hoped these projects will reduce or level out uneven high costs of electricity to different areas. The money is being used to construct badly needed roads and bridges across the state and to help meet the high cost of repairing existing roads. Civic centers are being built and projects funded to improve the quality of life in Alaskan communities. For instance, Alaska has created a subsidized home mortgage program called the Alaska Housing Finance Corporation. The program has helped more than 40,000 Alaskans to buy homes at below-market interest rates. The corporation handles about ninety percent of all mortgages arranged in the state. The state has also subsidized office construction and has created a program for obtaining state assisted business loans.

In the long run, there are three things that the majority of Alaskans hope to accomplish with the state's oil money. First, it is hoped that wise

Opposite: *Twelve pump stations along the 800-mile Alyeska Pipeline move oil through the forty-eight-inch-diameter pipe from the oilfields at Prudhoe Bay to the ice-free port of Valdez. About half of the pipeline is buried. In areas of permafrost, the pipeline is above ground, as in this area near Glennallen.*

investments will be made to get the most possible income from the principal that is invested. Second, there is strong support for investing in the development of renewable resources that will broaden Alaska's economic base, but not to the extent that it would cause overcapitalization. Third, it is hoped that development can occur on a scale that will not cause growth trends and population explosions that outpace the rate at which community improvements and environmental systems can be built to cope with them.

2. Land Regions

Alaska is so large and its climate and geography vary so widely that it is often thought of as six distinct land regions.

The Southeastern or Panhandle Region

Southeastern Alaska is a narrow strip of mainland and offshore islands sandwiched between northern British Columbia and the Pacific Ocean. It is most often called simply "Southeast" or "Southeastern" by Alaskans, as if it were a proper name rather than a description of a location. The beautiful and protected waterway that lies between the mainland and islands is known as the Inside Passage, where deepwater vessls can sail close to steep mountain walls. High, rugged coastal mountains—the highest coastal range in the world—rise sharply from the water's edge, and together with over 1000 islands, form many beautiful bays, fjords, and coves.

Much of Southeast is part of the Tongass National Forest, the largest national forest in America. The land is covered by massive stands of spruce, hemlock, and cedar. Most of the area is accessible only by water or by air, as the islands and mountainous terrain make highway construction impossible. Instead, a highly developed marine highway system efficiently provides transportation between the cities and small communities of Southeast. The ferries also provide connections with the cities of Prince Rupert, British Columbia, and Seattle, Washington. Only three cities, Skagway, Haines, and Hyder, are connected by land routes to the rest of the state.

15

The climate of Southeast is wet and mild, with warm winters and cool summers. The average summertime temperature is sixty degrees, with an occasional day in the eighties. During the winter the temperature averages twenty to forty degrees, seldom dropping below zero. Yearly precipitation ranges from twenty-six inches in Skagway to 227 inches in Little Port Walter on Baranof Island.

The rainy climate is something most people of Southeast take in stride. It can be a fiercely beautiful thing of gales and wind-whipped waves, or a gentle mist sifting over the land and drifting like a shroud through the spruce. But even those who do not like the rain agree that when the sun shines, Southeast is one of the most beautiful places on earth. The sun shines most often during the summer; the wettest season occurs in late fall. Snow, rain, and sunshine alternate during the spring and winter. Snowfall ranges from just over thirty inches to more than 200 inches in the mountains and around glaciers. At lower elevations in the southern third of the region, snows usually melt within a few days.

Nearly 60,000 people live in Southeast. Of these, nearly 45,000 reside in the five largest cities—Juneau, Ketchikan, Petersburg, Sitka, and Wrangell. The native population is comprised of Tlingit, Haida, and Tsimshian indians and numbers about 12,000 people. The highly developed totemic culture of these Indians is of major interest to travelers.

The four major industries in Southeast are lumbering, fishing, government, and tourism. The timber harvest from the dense forests of the region provides lumber for the pulp mills in Ketchikan and Sitka, and for the sawmills in Haines, Ketchikan, Metlakatla, Petersburg, and Wrangell. Fishing and fish processing is another mainstay of the economy and provides a living for a large segment of the population. The leading product of the fishing industry is salmon, followed by crab, shrimp, halibut, herring, and cod.

Juneau, Alaska's capital, is the center of Southeast's third largest industry—government. There is some question now as to whether this will be the case in coming years. In 1976, the Alaskan people voted to move their capital to a new site more centrally located in the state. A capital site selection committee chose Willow, a small town just north of Anchorage, as the target of the move, and plans were set in motion to build a brand new capital city at the base of the Talkeetna Mountains. In 1982, however, funding for the new capital was rejected by the people, and today the seat of government remains in Juneau. It is uncertain whether this is the end of the issue or if it will crop up again in future elections.

Tourism also contributes heavily to the economy and is becoming more and more important as a major source of income for the people of Southeast.

In addition to its picturesque towns and rugged natural beauty, Southeast offers several national parks and monuments. In Misty Fjords National Monument, the awe-inspiring grandeur of mountains and sea is breathtaking; in Admiralty Island National Monument, the perfect balance of a uniquely self-contained ecosystem can be seen and enjoyed. Glacier Bay National Park and Preserve, also in Southeast, boasts some of North America's most dramatic natural features, with active tidewater glaciers, ice-choked bays, lush rain forests, and abundant wildlife. Sitka National Historical Park offers a look into the rich frontier life of the past, as does the Klondike Gold Rush National Historical Park near Skagway.

Wildlife in Southeast includes whales, porpoises, harbor seals, mountain goats, brown and black bears, and over 200 species of birds, including a population of over 20,000 American bald eagles.

The Southcentral Region

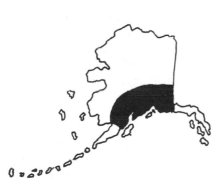

Southcentral Alaska is that area south of the rugged Alaska Range and is by far the most populous area in the state. Nearly three-fourths of all the people in Alaska live in Southcentral, which fronts on the Gulf of Alaska and includes Cook Inlet, the Kenai Peninsula, and Prince William Sound. The mountain range behind it, which forms an arc that parallels the coast, protects the region from the cold north winds. Because of this, Southcentral enjoys a relatively mild climate, with temperatures ranging from forty-five to seventy-five degrees in the summer, and from ten below zero to twenty degrees in the winter. Yearly precipitation ranges from 167 inches at Cordova on the Gulf of Alaska to eleven inches in Glennallen, inland from Valdez. Average annual precipitation in Anchorage is fifteen inches. Snowfall in Southcentral ranges from very heavy along the coastal areas exposed to gulf storms, to moderate in areas protected from the gulf by mountains. Thompson Pass, just north of Valdez, holds the state record for the most snowfall in a single season: 974.5 inches.

The major population center of Southcentral is the city of Anchorage. About sixty percent of all Alaskans reside here, and nearly three-fourths of Alaska's population lies within the Anchorage greater trading area.

Downtown Anchorage is a curious mixture of sleek modern high-rise buildings and small residential houses and apartment buildings. This view of Anchorage is looking north from the Delaney Park Strip.

Other major cities of Southcentral are Cordova, Homer, Kenai, Seldovia, Seward, and Valdez, which all lie along the coast, and Glennallen, Palmer, Soldotna, Talkeetna, and Wasilla, which lie inland.

Southcentral is known as a center of commerce and distribution for the rest of Alaska. Its major sources of revenue are government agencies, the oil industry, military bases, and transportation facilities. Fishing, farming, and tourism are also important.

Anchorage has been called the air crossroads of the world, and the Anchorage International Airport is indeed one of the busiest in the world. It serves Alaskan and United States domestic carriers as well as Orient- and Europe-bound foreign airlines operated over the Polar Route. Anchorage's Lake Hood is one of the world's largest seaplane bases, and Merrill Field, an airport used for general aviation, is the twenty-seventh busiest airport in the United States. There are six times as many pilots and twelve times as many private aircraft in Alaska as there are in any other state in the United States, and a good many of these pilots make their base in Southcentral.

There are also several strategic military establishments located near Anchorage. Elmendorf Air Force Base is located in Anchorage, as is Fort Richardson Army Base. Southcentral is the southern hub of Alaska's highway system, and the Alaska Marine Highway System operates its southwest branch in the Gulf of Alaska.

Oil exploration began in Southcentral in the mid 1950s, and extensive exploration has established that Cook Inlet's middle ground shoals contain major oil and gas fields. There are many drilling platforms located offshore in Cook Inlet. Several ammonia plants and oil refineries are now located near Kenai. There is a possibility of future oil industry impact near Homer with exploratory drilling in lower Cook Inlet.

Much of Alaska's farmland lies in the rich valleys of Southcentral. Although the growing season is only about 100 days, the long hours of daylight produce double-sized vegetables and berries, large-kerneled grain, and lush hay. The famous Matanuska Valley near Palmer and the Homer area on the Kenai Peninsula are two of the state's key farming centers. A new dairy farming experiment has begun recently near Knik, across the inlet from the city of Anchorage.

Southcentral Alaska is mountainous and forested. Beautiful green river valleys branch out from the relatively low-lying "bowl" around Cook Inlet. There are views of mountains in nearly every direction from almost any point in Southcentral. Six major mountain chains surround this area of the state. The Aleutian Range to the southwest, the Wrangell–St. Elias Range to the east, and the Alaska Range forming an arc to the west, north, and northeast contain some of the highest mountains in North America, including America's tallest peak, Mt. McKinley. The Chugach Mountains lie along the coast to the east and south; the Talkeetna Mountains rise to the north; and the Kenai Mountains cover the southeastern half of the Kenai Peninsula. Beautiful blue-green glaciers, winding fjords, and rounded emerald islands characterize the area around the coast. On the edges of Prince William Sound, abundant rain and snow nurtures a forest of spongy moss, silent and straight-growing Sitka spruce, and western hemlock. The Kenai Peninsula and the area inland from Anchorage supports thousands of acres of birch, aspen, white spruce, and spindly black spruce. Cottonwood is found near rivers and streams, and rolling meadows are blanketed with wildflowers for most of the summer.

The Chugach National Forest, the second largest national forest in America, provides thousands of acres of developed and undeveloped recreational opportunities, as does the Wrangell–St. Elias National Park and Preserve. Denali National Park and Preserve, which contains 20,320-foot Mt. McKinley, is the best known of all Alaska's national parks, and lies on the northern border of Southcentral. Lake Clark National Monument and Kenai Fjords National Monument are both located here, as is the Kenai National Wildlife Refuge, which contains a large concentration of moose. The moose are of record size, some with antler spreads in excess of six feet.

Also found in Southcentral are caribou, Dall sheep, mountain goats, and bear. Marine animals include harbor seals, sea otters, sea lions, porpoises, and killer and humpback whales. Trumpeter swans and colorful puffins are two unusual species of birds found in this region.

The Interior Region

The interior region of Alaska is a vast rolling upland containing isolated groups of mountains. The region lies between the Alaska Range to the south and the Brooks Range to the north. It extends from the Canadian border nearly to the Bering Sea. Much of the area is cut into many small mesas by broad river valleys and the numerous streams and tributaries of the Yukon River, which flows through the region in a westerly direction.

There is discontinuous permafrost throughout the interior region. Some of the northern sections have almost continuous permafrost, while southern areas have some south-sloping hillsides and river plains that are permafrost-free. Below elevations of 2000 feet, almost the entire interior region is covered with dense forests, ranging from large stands of white spruce, birch, and aspen on well-drained hillsides to thickets of scraggly black spruce on wet muskeg areas. Other dominant trees are the black cottonwood, poplar, western larch, and tamarack. Of the 28 million acres classified as commercial forest in Alaska, nearly 23 million acres lie in the interior. However, commercial lumbering in the interior has never been done on a large scale, mainly because of the inaccessibility of the vast roadless areas and the long period of time necessary for reforestation in the harsh climate.

Great extremes in temperature characterize the climate of the interior. Extreme cold, sometimes plunging to −72 degrees, is the norm from late November to mid–March. Rivers remain frozen from late October until breakup in late April or early May. Snow, lacking thaw or evaporation, usually accumulates all winter and is deep and fluffy despite the small amount of precipitation received in the region. Because of the dry climate, some people find the winter cold comfortable and invigorating; most find it at least tolerable. Summer temperatures can also be extreme. Daytime temperatures as high as ninety degrees may be followed by freezing nights. Yearly precipitation in the interior ranges from ten to fifteen inches, most of which comes in the form of summer showers.

The largest city in Alaska's interior is Fairbanks, which is also the second largest city in the state. There are about 60,000 people living in the Fairbanks greater area. Fairbanks is an important air transportation center and is the northern terminus of the Alaska Railroad. It is also the northern hub of the Alaskan road network. The Alaska, Richardson, and George Parks highways all have their northern terminus in Fairbanks, and secondary highways or narrow dirt roads lead from there to interior waterways and landing fields. Because of its excellent transportation facilities and its central location, Fairbanks is considered the gateway to the artic, and to the cities of Nome, Kotzebue, Point Hope, Point Barrow, and Prudhoe Bay. Other population centers in interior Alaska are Circle, Delta Junction, Eagle, Fort Yukon, McGrath, Nenana, North Pole, Ruby, Tanana, and Tok. There are dozens of native villages along the rivers in the western portion of the interior, and Indian villages dot the landscape in the central and eastern portions. These latter villages are home to the Athabascan Indians, some of whom remain hunters, trappers and fishermen, while others are now working in industry.

Mining contributes heavily to the economy of the interior. Gold production has increased in the past two decades, and there Is Increasing interest in the mining of other minerals as well, especially copper, lead, zinc, silver, and nickel. The state's only producing coal mine is the Usibelli Mine at Healy in the interior.

The Tanana Valley of interior Alaska is one of the state's major agricultural centers. Farm production includes hay, vegetables, fruits, and grains, particularly barley, which produces well during the relatively short growing season. Twenty-one daily hours of light during the summer produce grains that are extremely high in protein, and oversize but still very tender vegetables. Many farmers are also beginning to raise cattle for meat production. Fertilizer plants and grain storage bins are now being built in the Delta Junction area.

Travel through Alaska's interior reveals gold camps and dredges, working mines, and rollicking saloons. There are riverboat cruises, hot springs resorts, and native villages, where fish wheels can still be seen working in the mighty Yukon River. The Yukon-Charley Rivers National Monument and Preserve is located in the interior, as is Yukon Flats National Monument, a haven for millions of migratory waterfowl. Travel in the interior recalls Athabascan Indian history, gold rush days, the riverboat era, and the frontier spirit of an earlier America.

The Southwestern Region

Southwestern Alaska includes the Alaska Peninsula, the Aleutian Islands, and the Kodiak group of islands. The Alaska Peninsula is about 550 miles long. The Aleutian chain of islands extends westward an additional 1500 miles, separating the Pacific Ocean from the Bering Sea. The Aleutian Islands have the distinction of being both the westernmost point

and the easternmost point in the
United States. Pochnoi Point on
Semisopochnoi Island lies across the
180th meridian and is thus in the
Eastern Hemisphere.

Southwestern Alaska is mountainous and is subject to violent
storms which originate here and
affect the weather in Canada and the
rest of the United States. It is also
one of the largest volcanic chains in
the world. Two of the highest vol-
canoes, Mount Pavlov (8,900 feet) and Mount Veniaminof (8,400 feet),
rise from the Aleutian Island backbone. Southwestern Alaska, with the exception of Kodiak Island and some parts of the Alaska Peninsula, is
treeless. The climate is maritime, with cool, foggy summers and mild
winters.

There are about 8000 Aleut natives and 5000 military personnel who
live on military installations, at airports, and in the isolated supply and
fishing villages of the southwest region.

Kodiak, known as the king crab capital of the world, is the largest city
of Southwest and was the first permanent Russian settlement in Alaska.
Most of it has been rebuilt since giant tidal waves resulting from the Good
Friday earthquake destroyed much of the city and its economy in
1964.

Katmai National Monument on the Alaska Peninsula is one of the major tourist attractions in the state. It was here that, in 1912, Mt. Novarupta
exploded, forming the Valley of 10,000 Smokes. Also on the Alaska Peninsula is a volcanic crater nearly six miles wide and 2000 feet deep that attracts many visitors. The Kodiak National Wildlife Refuge, famous as the
home of the massive Kodiak brown bear, is located on the southwestern
two thirds of Kodiak Island.

There are no roads connecting southwestern Alaska to the rest of the
state. There are a few short local roads on Kodiak Island and on the Alaska
Peninsula near Iliamna, Old Iliamna, and King Salmon, but the only access to Southwest from the major population centers is by water or by air.
The Alaska Marine Highway System makes regular ferry stops at Kodiak
and Port Lions, and provides limited service to Chignik, Sand Point, King
Cove, Cold Bay, and Dutch Harbor.

The Western Region

Western Alaska lies west of the Interior and includes the Seward Peninsula, the Norton Sound area, and the Yukon and Kuskokwim river deltas. The Bristol Bay area and numerous coastal islands are included in this region as well.

Cool, foggy, rainy summers typify western Alaska. Average summertime temperatures range from the low forties to the low sixties. High winds and high humidity characterize the winters, which are only moderately cold, with temperatures ranging from five below to twenty-five degrees in the north, and from zero to thirty-five degrees in the south.

Many of Alaska's natives live in the western region. Native villages are scattered across the land in locations where families have fished and trapped for generations.

There are thousands of lakes and ponds in western Alaska and two mighty rivers—the muddy Kuskokwim and the myriad channels and sloughs that make up the mouth of the Yukon. The Woods-Tikchik area in the southern portion of the region is considered one of the most scenic areas in the state because of its beautiful parallel glacial lakes. This area is the largest glaciated region in North America, although there are no glaciers now present.

The Seward Peninsula is characterized by broad convex hills and ridges surmounted by more rugged mountain groups, and the entire area is underlain with permafrost. Most of the vegetation in this area is tundra, and grasses, sedges, mosses, and lichens cover the ground. On the western highlands to the south of Nome are the Selawik Hills, low, rolling mountains with northeast trending ridges. Further south, separating the Yukon–Kuskokwim Delta from the Bristol Bay area, are the Kilbuck and Ahklun mountains and the more extensive Kuskokwim Mountains. Areas in the south of western Alaska have only some discontinuous permafrost, and the thickly forested hillsides in the Bristol Bay area are classified as forest lands. On the delta side of the mountains, stands of white spruce and balsam poplar grow upriver on the Yukon, and birch and spruce have a good foothold inland along the Kuskokwim.

Nome and Bethel are the region's largest cities. After the big gold rush at the turn of the century, Nome settled down to become the principal trading and mining center for the Seward Peninsula. Gold dredges still operate in the Nome area, principally for the benefit of tourists, and rich copper deposits are now beginning to be developed. A large community of natives, famous for ivory-carving skills, lives on the outskirts of Nome. Bethel is the heart city of the Yukon–Kuskokwim Delta and serves as the main distribution center for native villages throughout the area. Goods are shipped to Bethel on large barges or flown in by commercial airliner, and from there are transported to the many native villages by bush plane or small boats.

Dillingham, separated from the delta by mountains, is the principal city of the Bristol Bay area. Like Bethel, it serves many villages inland from the bay by distributing supplies. It is also a major center for fish processing.

Most residents of western Alaska live a subsistence lifestyle supplemented by income from commercial fishing for salmon. Tourism is also becoming increasingly important, and there are now many hunting and fishing lodges and guide services throughout the entire southern half of western Alaska, particularly in the Bristol Bay area.

The Arctic Region

The northern third of Alaska lies within the Arctic Circle and is Alaska's only true polar area. The Brooks Range, which runs from the Canadian border to the Chukchi Sea just south of Kotzebue, separates the arctic region of Alaska from the Interior. This vast range is 720 miles long and contains nine different groups of mountains, the highest and widest being the Romanzoi Mountains in the northeastern portion of the region. The north slope is the vast coastal plain, which slopes gently downward from the foothills of the Brooks Range to the edge of the Arctic Ocean. Most of the area is underlain with permafrost up to 2000 feet thick and is covered with tundra. Vast deposits of oil and gas lie beneath the tundra, as do large deposits of coal, and oil exploration is continuing.

The winter climate, although extreme in comparison to the lower forty-eight, is actually less severe in the Arctic than in Alaska's interior region, thanks to the ameliorating effects of the Arctic Ocean. In Barrow, the northernmost city in Alaska, the temperature ranges from thirty to forty degrees in summer, and from fifteen below to eighteen below in the winter. Winter winds, however, sometimes counter this effect with chill factors to below −100 degrees. In the Arctic, as in the Interior, conditions are right for temperature inversions during periods of no wind, and these often occur throughout the winter, trapping cold air on the ground and accentuating air pollution in cities, where steam and smoke from heating systems cannot escape into the atmosphere. In the Arctic, which is very dry, about five inches of precipitation remain on the ground as snow for eight or nine months of the year. The ground never thaws more than two feet below the surface, so trees cannot grow.

The Arctic Circle is that latitude at which, on the day of the summer solstice, the sun never sets; likewise, on the day of the winter solstice, it never rises. In northern portions of arctic Alaska there is a period of about two months during the summer when the sun shines continually without setting, and the thawed ground becomes thickly carpeted with low grasses and wildflowers. There is also a period of about two months during the winter when the only light to be seen is that of the moon and stars and the beautiful color displays of the northern lights in the night sky.

The majority of the people in the Arctic are native Alaskans who rely on reindeer herding, hunting, and fishing for their subsistence. Many are adept at jade and ivory carving as well as other native arts and crafts. Temporary work, usually for the government or in construction, is often needed to supplement the subsistence lifestyle.

Tourism is of increasing importance to the economy as the picturesque native life attracts a growing number of visitors. There is now regularly scheduled airline service to most major communities in the Arctic. There are no roads throughout any portion of the region except the north slope haul road, so for transportation in most areas the people still depend on boats in summer, and snowmachines or dogsleds in winter, and planes year-round. Equipment and supplies are brought in by barge from the lower forty-eight once a year for the people in the coastal villages and for the oil drilling operations along the shoreline.

There are millions of acres in arctic Alaska that have been set aside by the federal government as monuments, preserves, and wildlife refuges. Here can be found the Gates of the Arctic National Monument, one of the most completely unspoiled wilderness areas left in America. Also in this region are Kobuk Valley National Park and Preserve, Noatak National Preserve, and the Arctic National Wildlife Refuge, which alone contains 18 million acres.

Wildlife in the region is very plentiful. Two of the largest caribou herds, the porcupine herd and the western arctic herd, make their home on the tundra and range over hundreds of miles. Moose, wolves, bears, foxes, and lynx are found here as are many smaller mammals such as

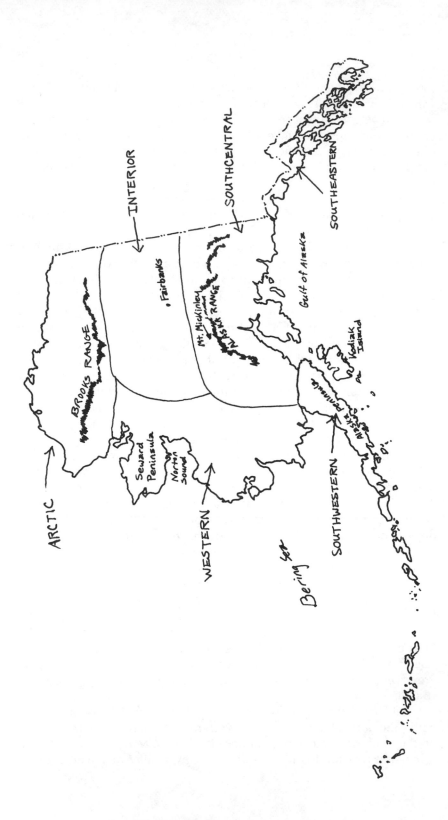

wolverine, weasel, otter, snowshoe hares, and mice and lemmings. Musk oxen have been reintroduced to the Arctic from a herd started on Nunivak Island, and now range near Cape Thompson on the seacoast and on the arctic slope near Kavik.

The principal cities of the Arctic are Kotzebue and Barrow. Barrow is only 800 miles from the North Pole and is the northernmost inhabited village in North America.

Opposite: *The six land regions.*

3. Transportation

The highway system.

Alaska's Highway System

There are only about 10,000 miles of road in Alaska, most of which lie south of the Yukon River and east of the Alaska Peninsula. About 3000 miles of the highways in Alaska are paved, 6000 miles of road are graded and graveled, and about 1000 miles are unimproved. Large areas of the state can be reached only by water or air. Haines, Skagway, and Hyder are the only cities in Southeast that connect by land to the rest of the state. Likewise, the entire western half of Alaska can be reached only by boat or by plane. There is only one land bridge over the Yukon River and only one highway in the entire northern portion of the state. The Dalton Highway to Prudhoe Bay, formerly called the North Slope Haul Road, is the only northern land link with the population centers to the south.

The Alaska Highway is the only land link to the lower forty-eight states. Much of it lies in Canada. The highway is 1523 miles long from mile 0 in Dawson Creek, British Columbia, to its northern terminus in Fairbanks. Almost all of it is now paved. There are still a few hundred miles of the Canadian section that are not paved; however, the unpaved portion is considered the finest gravel road to be found anywhere. The entire Alaska section is paved. The whole length of the highway is open and passable year round, and during very bad weather the Canadian Government supplies patrols to convey travelers from point to point.

Driving the Alaska Highway is somewhat different than traveling in the lower forty-eight states. Service stations dot the highway on both the Alaskan and Canadian portions, but power and water hookups are not always available en route. About 300 miles per day is a realistic pace and includes time to stop at points of interest along the way. The trip from Seattle to Anchorage via the Alaskan Highway is 2484 miles and averages five driving days. It is a good idea to reduce speed when approaching oncoming traffic on unpaved stretches to minimize the impact of flying gravel. Headlights should be turned on when the road is dusty to present high visibility to oncoming motorists. Watch the signs carefully; there are places where frost heaves have created sudden bumps or dips in the pavement, which can give a pretty good jolt when taken with too much speed.

Alaskans are a rather casual people, so a minimal amount of dress clothing will be needed. Most Alaskans wear comfortable clothing such as jeans or slacks. A light- to medium-weight jacket should be included, as evenings are usually cool. A raincoat is a must. The best way not to need your raingear is to have it along.

Vehicle insurance must be in effect to enter Alaska, Canada, and the Yukon Territory. Uninsured vehicles will be turned back. Canadian customs officials will require vehicle registration cards or proof of title.

Passports are not required of U.S. citizens when entering Canada, but proof of residency or citizenship, such as a birth certificate or driver's license, will be needed. Canadian law requires travelers at the border to show proof of sufficient funds to cover travel costs, including possible breakdowns. Owners of pets traveling through Canada are required to have with them a valid health certificate issued by a licensed veterinarian. Handguns are not permitted in Canada and will be sent back to the owner's home address at the owner's expense.

A very valuable publication to carry along both to and within Alaska is *The Milepost*, a book put out by the Alaska Northwest Publishing Company, which is updated each year and contains mile-by-mile information on all highways within Alaska, the Alaska Highway, and other access roads and highways in Canada. This publication can be obtained at some larger bookstores in the lower forty-eight or can be obtained by writing:

Alaska Northwest Publishing Company
Box 4-EEE
Dept. MP86
Anchorage, Alaska 99509

The price of the book is $11.95 plus $1.00 postage for fourth class or $3.00 postage and handling for first class.

The Alaska Railroad

The only government-owned railroad in the United States operates in Alaska. Its southern terminals are located in Whittier, on Prince William Sound, and in Seward on the Kenai Peninsula. The state of Alaska is in the process of buying the railroad from the federal government, so perhaps before long it will no longer be government-owned. The railroad spans the wilderness of the last frontier, stretching northward 470 miles to its present northern terminus in Fairbanks. The only other rail service in Alaska, the narrow-gauge White Pass and Yukon route from Skagway to Whitehorse, suspended service in 1982. Although it may someday reopen, there is no date set for the immediate future.

The Alaska Railroad was begun in 1915 to provide a means of transportation and freight service between the coastal ocean ports and the interior mining areas. It was completed in 1923, when then-president Warren G. Harding drove the official gold spike at Nenana to signify completion. The main track ran from Seward to the Tanana River at Nenana, with branch lines to the coal fields at Sutton in the Matanuska Valley. Later the track was extended to Fairbanks.

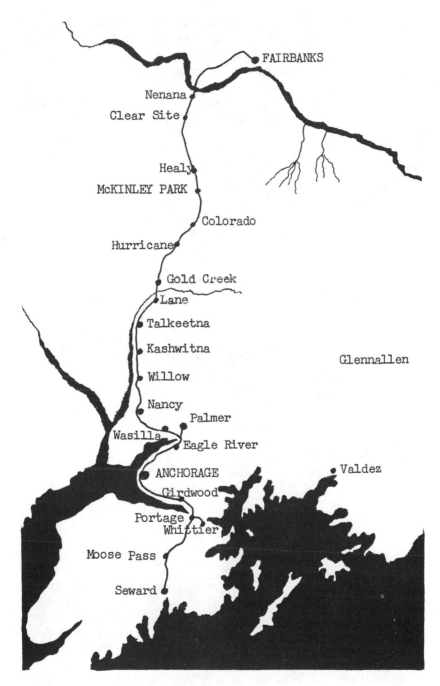

The railway system.

Today, there is freight service over its entire length, and regular passenger service between Anchorage and Fairbanks. A vehicle rail shuttle service operates between Portage and Whittier. Since the railroad is the only means of transportation for many people who live along its length, certain trains make many stops to pick up or drop off passengers, mail, or freight. The rail route winds through canyons and climbs mountain passes, and is probably one of the few trains in the world that will still stop when flagged to pick up passengers in the most unlikely places. Occasionally the Alaska Railroad will run special trains at the request of various groups or organizations.

There are four passenger trains operating on the Alaska Railroad between Anchorage and Fairbanks. Trains #1 and #2 are the Denali Express and the Anchorage Express. Both travel daily between Fairbanks and Anchorage, with one stop at Denali National Park. Both offer full dining and beverage service, comfortable reclining seats, and scenic dome car service for viewing the magnificent scenery. They are staffed by high school students trained to answer questions and point out locations of interest along the way. Reservations are required and should be made at least two weeks in advance. Train #1 leaves Fairbanks at 10:30 a.m., arrives in Denali Park at 1:55 p.m., and in Anchorage at 8:00 p.m. Train #2 leaves Anchorage at 8:30 a.m., arrives in Denali Park at 2:35 p.m., and in Fairbanks at 6:00 p.m. Trains #3 and #4 make all stops along the route and also make flag stops. They are ideal for backpackers, fishermen, and mountain climbers. Train #3 operates southbound on Thursday and Sunday, and train #4 operates northbound on Wednesday and Saturday. During the winter, the trains operate weekly. Passenger service is not regularly scheduled to Seward, but trains are operated on an irregular basis for special events.

Fares, though subject to change without notice, are currently as follows:

Anchorage to Denali Park:	one way	$ 48.50
	round trip	$ 97.00
Fairbanks to Denali Park:	one way	$ 26.25
	round trip	$ 52.50
Anchorage to Fairbanks:	one way	$ 69.75
	round trip	$139.50

The rail service between Anchorage, Portage, and Whittier is a shuttle service for passengers and vehicles that is operated jointly by the Alaska Railroad and the Alaska Department of Transportation. Train departures from Portage are timed to meet arrivals and departures of vessels of the marine highway system which connect Whittier and Valdez. Vehicles traveling by rail must board and disembark at Portage. There are loading

The distinctive design of an Alaska Railroad passenger car in Seward. The railroad spans the wilderness from its southern terminus in Seward to its northern terminus in Fairbanks. It no longer provides regularly scheduled service to Seward from Anchorage, but makes special trips for certain scheduled events throughout the summer.

ramps located beside the Seward Highway at Portage, and train tickets can be purchased from ticket sellers at the loading ramps. Reservations are needed for the ferry but are not accepted for this portion of the rail service. Passengers with confirmed ferry reservations are given priority on the first shuttle. Passengers without vehicles may return to Anchorage only on the last trip of the day between Whittier and Portage.

For further information, write the Alaska Railroad, Pouch 7-2111, Anchorage AK 99510.

The Alaska Marine Highway System

Because so many Alaskan communities are separated from one another by water, travel by ship is a necessity in many parts of the state. Alaska maintains an extensive marine highway system, extending over 2200 miles. The marine highway links communities throughout Alaska and provides surface connections with Prince Rupert, British Columbia, and Seattle, Washington.

From the decks of Alaska's ferryliners, voyagers can see giant glaciers, towering mountain peaks, and wild coastlines. In the waters, sea lions and porpoises are visible, and occasionally whales surface to blow.

Facilities on all the ferries include sightseeing solariums, a cocktail lounge, and a dining room. Four southeast ferries and one southwest ferry also have passenger staterooms.

Pets are allowed on the ferries, but owners are required to have in their possession a valid health certificate for each animal. The animals must be in suitable containers, must be cared for by their owners, and must remain on the car deck. Passengers are allowed on the car deck only when accompanied by the purser during designated periods while the ferry is underway or while the ferry is docked.

There is no limit on the amount of baggage that may be transported in vehicles on the vessel, but foot passengers may bring hand luggage only.

Reservations are required for vehicles and staterooms on all southeast ferries, and passenger reservations are required on all sailings to and from Seattle. Reservations are required for vehicles, staterooms, and passengers on all ferries operating in the southwest segment of the system. It is recommended that reservations be obtained as far in advance as possible since the ferries are very popular during the summer and tickets are often sold out quite early. For Seattle sailings it may be necessary to obtain summer reservations as early as January, since space is sometimes sold out by February. Full payment is due for confirmed reservations at least forty-five days prior to sailing. Personal checks are not accepted unless they are written on an Alaskan bank. Tickets can either be mailed to your home address or they can be held for you at your departure point, but in either case, the tickets must be prepaid.

Three types of fares are charged on the ferries:

(1) Vehicle fares depend on the size of the vehicle and how much room it will take up on the ferry.

(2) Passenger fares vary with the age of the passenger. Adults pay full fare, children under twelve pay half fare and children under six ride free.

(3) Cabin fares are charged according to the type of accommodations and vary with each vessel. Cabins are sold as a unit, not on a per berth basis, although some ferries do have dormitory rooms which are sold on a per berth basis. Passengers who do not wish to reserve a stateroom or dormitory berth are allowed to bed down in deck chairs or sleeping bags on deck except on Seattle sailings. There are public bathroom facilities available for these passengers.

The ferries operate year-round in two distinct seasons. The summer season lasts from May 1 to September 30, and sailings during this time are both more frequent and more expensive. The winter season begins on October 30 and lasts until April 30. Sailings are less frequent during this time

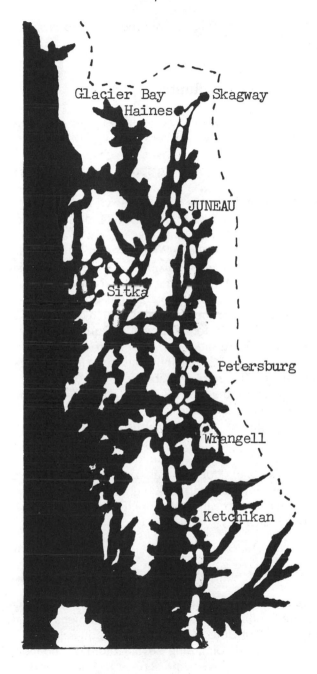

The Southeast ferry routes.

of the year, but fares are considerably reduced and crowds are almost nonexistent.

Southeast Alaska Ferry Routes

There are nine ferries presently operating in two noninterconnecting segments of the marine highway system. Seven of these ferries operate in southeast Alaska, where they connect the cities of Seattle and Prince Rupert to Wrangell, Ketchikan, Petersburg, Sitka, Juneau, Haines, and Skagway.

The M/V Columbia is the largest ferry, with capacity for 1000 passengers, 180 vehicles, and berths for 324 persons. The Columbia operates once a week between the cities of Seattle and Skagway.

Three ferries operate between Prince Rupert, British Columbia, and Skagway. All ports receive service six days per week except Sitka, which has service once per week. The three ferries are the M/V Malaspina and the M/V Matanuska with capacity for 750 passengers, 120 vehicles, and berths for 280 persons, and the ferry Taku, which carries 500 passengers, 105 vehicles, and has berths for 100 persons. During the summer months another ferry, the M/V Aurora, operates a route between Prince Rupert and Juneau. The Aurora is 235 feet long, has room for 47 vehicles and carries 250 passengers. There are no cabins on the Aurora.

Two smaller ferries, the M/V LeConte and the Chilkat, provide connection for many small towns and villages to Ketchikan and Juneau. The LeConte operates in the northern portion, providing connections to Juneau, and the Chilkat in the southern portion, providing connections to Ketchikan. Some of the small communities serviced by these ferries are Metlakatla, Hollis, Kake, Hoonah, Tenakee, Angoon, and Pelican. The LeConte is 235 feet long and carries 47 vehicles and 250 passengers. The Chilkat is 99 feet long and carries 15 vehicles and 75 passengers. Neither of these ferries has cabins.

Southwest Alaska Ferry Routes

There are two ferries presently operating in the Prince William Sound area, called the Southwest route. The ferry Tustumena provides regular service to Seward, Port Lions, Kodiak, Homer, and Seldovia, and limited service to Chignik, Sand Point, King Cove, Cold Bay, and Dutch Harbor. It provides supplementary weekend service to Valdez and Cordova via the Columbia Glacier. The Tustumena is 296 feet long and carries 220 passengers and 20 vehicles. There are 27 cabins on the Tustumena.

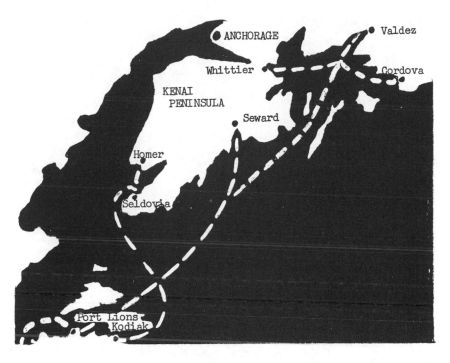

The Southwest ferry routes.

The M/V Bartlett provides daily connections between Cordova, Valdez, and Whittier with a tie-in to the Alaska Railroad at Whittier. The Bartlett is 193 feet long, carries 170 passengers and 38 vehicles, and has no cabins.

Ferry Rates

Schedules of ferry rates and sailings can be obtained by writing to the main office of the Alaska Marine Highway System, Pouch R, Juneau, Alaska 99811. For a recorded message that gives details on each vessel's current sailing times, including any possible delays, you dial (907) 465-3940. To order schedules and rates by phone, call (907) 465-3941.

Cabin rates vary according to the accommodations available on each ferry and the distance between ports. Sample rates for a four-berth cabin with a sitting room are given below.

Southeast Alaska

Seattle to Prince Rupert	$129.00
Seattle to Skagway	$202.00
Prince Rupert to Ketchikan	$ 40.00
Ketchikan to Wrangell	$ 40.00
Wrangell to Petersburg	$ 40.00
Petersburg to Sitka	$ 45.00
Petersburg to Juneau	$ 45.00
Sitka to Juneau	$ 45.00
Juneau to Haines	$ 40.00
Haines to Skagway	$ 40.00

Rates for a two-berth cabin:

Seattle to Prince Rupert	$ 83.00
Seattle to Skagway	$131.00
Prince Rupert to Ketchikan	$ 27.00
Ketchikan to Wrangell	$ 27.00
Wrangell to Petersburg	$ 27.00
Petersburg to Sitka	$ 29.00
Petersburg to Juneau	$ 29.00
Sitka to Juneau	$ 29.00
Juneau to Haines	$ 27.00
Haines to Skagway	$ 27.00

Rates for dormitory rooms:

Seattle to Prince Rupert	$ 42.00
Seattle to Skagway	$ 66.00
Prince Rupert to Ketchikan	$ 14.00
Ketchikan to Wrangell	$ 14.00
Wrangell to Petersburg	$ 14.00
Petersburg to Sitka	$ 15.00
Petersburg to Juneau	$ 15.00
Sitka to Juneau	$ 15.00
Juneau to Haines	$ 14.00
Haines to Skagway	$ 14.00

Three-berth cabins and four-berth cabins without sitting rooms are also available.

Southwest Alaska

Four-berth cabins, no facilities:

Seward to Port Lions	$ 65.00
Port Lions to Kodiak	$ 30.00

Kodiak to Homer	$ 59.00
Homer to Seldovia	$ 30.00
Kodiak to Seward	$ 65.00
Seward to Cordova	$ 59.00
Cordova to Valdez	$ 41.00
Seward to Valdez	$ 59.00

There are also two-berth cabins and dormitory rooms available on the ferry Tustumena. The shuttle ferry Bartlett, which sails between Whittier and Valdez, has no cabins.

Rates for vehicles on the ferry depend on the size of the vehicle. Sample rates for a vehicle up to and including nineteen feet are as given below:

Southeast Alaska

Seattle to Ketchikan	$387.00
Seattle to Skagway	$547.00
Prince Rupert to Ketchikan	$ 67.00
Ketchikan to Wrangell	$ 65.00
Wrangell to Petersburg	$ 37.00
Petersburg to Sitka	$ 82.00
Petersburg to Juneau	$ 82.00
Sitka to Juneau	$ 82.00
Juneau to Haines	$ 54.00
Haines to Skagway	$ 21.00

Southwest Alaska

Seward to Port Lions	$120.00
Port Lions to Kodiak	$ 34.00
Kodiak to Homer	$100.00
Homer to Seldovia	$ 23.00
Kodiak to Seward	$120.00
Seward to Cordova	$102.00
Cordova to Valdez	$ 59.00
Valdez to Whittier	$ 70.00

Sample passenger fares are as follows:

Southeast Alaska

Seattle to Ketchikan	$126.00
Seattle to Skagway	$188.00
Prince Rupert to Ketchikan	$ 23.00

Ketchikan to Wrangell	$ 22.00
Wrangell to Petersburg	$ 13.00
Petersburg to Sitka	$ 26.00
Petersburg to Juneau	$ 26.00
Sitka to Juneau	$ 32.00
Juneau to Haines	$ 19.00
Haines to Skagway	$ 9.00

Southwest Alaska

Seward to Port Lions	$ 37.00
Port Lions to Kodiak	$ 12.00
Kodiak to Homer	$ 32.00
Homer to Seldovia	$ 9.00
Kodiak to Seward	$ 37.00
Seward to Cordova	$ 43.00
Cordova to Valdez	$ 20.00
Seward to Valdez	$ 43.00
Valdez to Whittier	$ 42.00

Time Between Ports

A general idea of the time it takes to get from one port to another is necessary when planning a vacation in Alaska. Many ferry stops are a considerable distance from one another, and time en route is a major consideration when deciding whether to ride the ferry or to fly. Detailed schedules of sailing times throughout the summer are necessary when making reservations and are available from the Marine Highway System. Given below are sample times to give a general planning idea of how much time is involved between various ports. The times given can vary as much as two hours, depending on which direction the ferry is going and which ferry is being used. Times are the number of hours between departure from one port until departure from the next. The ferries are docked only long enough for passengers and vehicles to disembark and for others to board.

Southeast Alaska

Seattle to Prince Rupert	16 hours
Seattle to Skagway	50 hours
Prince Rupert to Ketchikan	7 hours
Ketchikan to Wrangell	7 hours
Wrangell to Petersburg	4 hours
Petersburg to Sitka	3 hours

Petersburg to Juneau	9 hours
Sitka to Juneau	14 hours
Juneau to Haines	6 hours
Haines to Skagway	1 hour

Southwest Alaska

Seward to Port Lions	14 hours
Port Lions to Kodiak	5 hours
Kodiak to Homer	12 hours
Homer to Seldovia	2 hours
Kodiak to Seward	16 hours
Seward to Cordova	12 hours
Cordova to Valdez	6 hours
Seward to Valdez	15 hours
Valdez to Whittier	8 hours

Air Travel*

The Federal Aviation Administration reports that there are over 10,000 registered pilots and nearly 8000 registered aircraft in the State of Alaska. This is not so surprising when you consider that the only means of transportation to many parts of the state, especially rural areas, is by air. Many people living in the bush depend on aircraft not only for their means of getting from one place to another, but also for their groceries, mail, and nearly everything else they cannot supply for themselves. Almost every Alaskan community has an airport or landing field and most have at least one air taxi operator. Even with its much smaller population, Alaska ranks third in the nation in the number of airports it maintains.

Most scheduled carriers and many air taxi operators have brochures describing their route system. Reservations can be made directly or through a travel agent. The large interstate airlines—Alaska, American, Markair (formerly Wien Air Alaska), Northwest, United, and Western— use jets that range from DC-8s to 747s. Other commercial air transport within Alaska is generally either jet or turboprop aircraft, but some smaller air taxi operators use single or twin-engine prop planes on wheels, skis, or floats. The following is a listing of air taxi operators in Alaska.

*For information on flying your own plane through Alaska, see Chapter 7.

Air Taxi Services

Anchorage:

Aero Tech Flight Service
1100 Merrill Field Drive
Anchorage AK 99501

Charters to anywhere in the state.
Operates out of Merrill field.

Alaska Aeronautical Industries
Box 6067 Airport Annex
Anchorage AK 99502

This is a commuter service to Kenai,
Soldotna, Homer, Kodiak, Seward,
Valdez, Cordova and Denali.

Alaska Air Guides
327 East Fireweed Lane
Anchorage AK 99503

Floatplane charters all over Alaska.
Operates out of Lake Hood near
the Anchorage International Airport.

Alaska Air Service
Box 6167 Airport Annex
Anchorage AK 99502

This service has single and multiengine land planes and float planes
for charter.

Alaska Bush Carrier
David Klosterman
4801 Aircraft Drive
Anchorage AK 99502

Air taxi service to fishing camps
in the Deshka and Kenai River
area. Float trips, hunting and
photography in area.

Alaska North Flying Service
Box 6323
Anchorage AK 99502

Float equipped aircraft for fishing,
hunting and flightseeing. Charter
services.

Alaska Travel Air
Box 6012
Anchorage AK 99502

Sportfishing, hunting, flightseeing
and photography trips. Charters to
many areas of Alaska.

Alaska West Air Tours
P.O. Box 6651
Anchorage AK 99502

Services tailored to fit your plans:
camping, sportfishing, photography,
wildlife excursions, etc.

Big Red's Flying Service
Box 6281
Anchorage AK 99502

Charters on wheels or floats for
sportfishing and hunting, camping,
wildlife photography, or floating.

Birchwood Air Service
Box B
Chugiak AK 99567

Flightseeing tours all over Alaska
including Denali, Columbia Glacier,
and the Kenai Peninsula.

Bran-Air Alaska
Box 6128 Airport Annex
Anchorage AK 99502

Flying photography and wildlife tours and sportfishing and hunting charters.

Bush Pilots, Inc.
Box 6389
Anchorage AK 99502

River raft trips, fly-in wilderness lodges for fishing and hunting, and photo safaris.

Era Helicopters
6160 South Airpark Drive
Anchorage AK 99502

Charter service for both helicopters and fixed-wing aircraft. Contract basis.

Evergreen Helicopters, Inc.
Box 578
Anchorage AK 99510

Both helicopters and fixed-wing aircraft are available for flightseeing and photography.

Jet Alaska
6160 South Alrpark Drive
Anchorage AK 99502

An air taxi, jet charter and air ambulance service.

Ketchum Air Service
2708 Aspen Drive
Anchorage AK 99503

Based at Lake Hood adjacent to the Anchorage International Airport.

Rust's Flying Service
Box 6325
Anchorage AK 99502

Charter service for fly-in camping, sport hunting, and sportfishing. Also float trips.

Sea Airmotive, Inc.
Box 6003 Airport Annex
Anchorage AK 99502

Both scheduled and charter service for sportfishing and flightseeing. Helicopters and fixed-wing aircraft.

Barrow:

Cape Smythe Air Service
Box 549
Barrow AK 99723

Serves villages throughout the Arctic including Barter Island, Deadhorse, Kotzebue, Point Hope, and Anaktuvuk Pass.

Bethel:

Bush Air
Box 100
Bethel AK 99559

Serves many camps, lodges, and lakes for sportfishing, hunting, and flightseeing.

Bettles:

Brooks Range Aviation
General Delivery
Bettles AK 99726

Charter service with three planes, a Beaver, Cessna 185 on floats, and a Cessna 206 on wheels.

Cordova:

Chisum Flying Service
Box 1288
Cordova AK 99574

Both helicopter and fixed-wing aircraft on wheels and floats.

Kennedy Air Service, Inc.
Box 909
Cordova AK 99574

Wheel- and float-equipped aircraft for charter.

Denali National Park:

Denali Wilderness Air
Box 82
Denali National Park AK
    99755

Flightseeing and bush pilot tours of Denali National Park. Fly in to remote lodge for wildlife photography.

Golden North Air Service
Box 9
Cantwell AK 99729

Wilderness camping and fly-in sportfishing. Flightseeing tours of Denali National Park.

Dillingham:

Yute Air Alaska, Inc.
Box 180
Dillingham AK 99576

Both scheduled and charter trips into bush Alaska. Many remote lodges for hunting and fishing in area.

Eagle:

Tatonduk Flying Service
P.O. Box 55
Eagle AK 99738

Air charter for sportfishing, gold panning, wilderness camping, and float trips.

Fairbanks:

Air Logistics of Alaska
1915 Donald Avenue
Fairbanks AK 99701

Twenty-two helicopters for flightseeing trips to goldmining towns and fishing camps. Groups of thirteen anywhere in the state.

Air North
Box 60054
Fairbanks AK 99706

A scheduled air carrier serving most points in Northern Alaska. Also Juneau and Whitehorse, Yukon.

Alaska Air Charter
Box 80507
Fairbanks AK 99708

Floatplane service to remote lakes with flightseeing tours throughout Alaska and Brooks ranges.

Arctic Circle Air Service, Inc.
Douglas Butler
Box 60049
Fairbanks AK 99706

Scheduled passengers and freight between Fairbanks and Fort Yukon. Also have wheels, floats, skis and multiengine for hunters, hikers, and tourists.

Frontier Flying Service, Inc.
3820 University Avenue
Fairbanks AK 99701

Scheduled service to Bettles and Anaktuvuk Pass and charter flights in Alaska and western Canada.

Hardy M. Smith, Registered
   Guide
Box 5153
North Pole AK 99705

Flightseeing tours of Brooks Range, Alaska Range and Denali National Park.

Larry's Flying Service
Box 2348
Fairbanks AK 99707

Scheduled service to Denali National Park. Charter services anywhere in Alaska.

Nenana Air Service, Inc.
Box 296
Nenana AK 99670

Air taxi operator serving the Nenana and Denali area.

Wright Air Service, Inc.
Box 60142
Fairbanks AK 99701

Arctic Circle tours and Alaska bush adventures. Photo excursions to Mt. McKinley.

Fort Yukon:

Air North
Box 60054
Fairbanks AK 99706

Air charter service for fishermen, hunters, backpackers, and float trips. Both land and floatplanes.

Galena:

Galena Air Service
Box 188
Galena AK 99741

Scheduled flights from Anchorage. Serves Ruby, Koyukuk, Nulato and several other villages. Ski aircraft.

Glennallen:

Ellis Air Taxi
Box 106
Glennallen AK 99588

Charter flights into Wrangell Mountains. Sportfishing and boating on area lakes.

Sportsman Flying Service
Gulkana Air Service
Box 31
Glennallen AK 99588

Logistical support of mountaineering parties in Wrangell Mountains. Float, wheel, skis, or amphibian for charter.

Gustavus/Glacier Bay:

Glacier Bay Airways
Box 1
Gustavus AK 99826

Bases at Juneau and Glacier Bay for air taxi service to all points in Southeast. Hunting and fishing packages.

Haines:

Air America, Inc.
P.O. Box 2321
Juneau AK 99803

Passenger service and flightseeing tours out of Haines, Hoonah, Juneau and Skagway. Hunting and fishing.

L.A.B. Flying Service
Box 272
Haines AK 99827

Base at Haines airport for flying tours anywhere in Southeast. Planes are amphibian or conventional wheel.

Homer:

Homer Air
Box 302
Homer AK 99603

Air charters for fishing, clam digging, and beachcombing. Seat fares to Jakalof, Seldovia and Port Graham.

Maritime Helicopters, Inc.
Box 357
Homer AK 99603

Tours to Augustine Island, Harding Ice Field, and Barren Islands. Photo trips to McNeil River bear sanctuary.

Iliamna:

Talarik Creek Air Taxi
Box 68
Illiamna AK 99606

Serves the Iliamna Lake area where there are many lodges and fishing camps. Based at Talarik Creek Lodge.

Juneau:

Channel Flying, Inc.
2601 Channel Drive
Juneau AK 99801

Multiengine amphibious charter to all parts of Southeast, British Columbia, and Yukon Territory.

L.A.B. Flying Service
Box 2201
Juneau AK 99803

Seventeen scheduled flights daily to several Southeast cities. Easy connections with major airline flights.

Ward Air
1873 Ward Simmons Dr.,
  Suite 5118
Juneau AK 99801

Amphibious air taxi operation for many locations in Southeast.

Katmai National Park:

Katmai Air
Box 175
King Salmon AK 99613

Charter service with floatplanes for access to sportfishing locations in Katmai.

Kenai:

Andy's Flying Service, Inc.
Box 4324
Kenai AK 99611

Flightseeing charters and fishing, clam digging, and photo expeditions.

Kenai Floatplane Service
Box 152
Kenai AK 99611

Air charters for flightseeing or other activities on floats, wheels, or skis.

Ketchikan:

Ketchikan Air Service, Inc.
Box 6900
Ketchikan AK 99901

This service has scheduled flights to Hyder, Alaska, and Stewart, B.C., to view old gold mining area.

Revilla Flying Service
1427 Tongass Avenue
Ketchikan AK 99901

Flights to forest service cabins and fishing lakes in Tongass and Misty Fjords.

Southeast Alaska Airlines, Inc.
1515 Tongass Avenue
Ketchikan AK 99901

Charter transportation to logging camps, villages, resorts, hunting and fishing lodges, and mining camps.

Taquan Air Service
P.O. Box 600
Metlakatla AK 99926

Regular service between Ketchikan and Metlakatla. Charter service to most of Southeast and B.C.

Temsco Helicopters
Box 5057
Ketchikan AK 99901

Two bases—one in Petersburg and
the other in Wrangell. Year-round
service.

Tyee Airlines
Box 8331
Ketchikan AK 99901

Regular service to Craig, Klawock,
Hydaburg, Annette Island, Yes Bay,
and Bell Island. Also charters.

Westflight Aviation
Box 6440
Ketchikan AK 99901

Serving the Waterfall Resort and all
Alaska, Canada, and U.S. with
Cessna Citation Jet Charter Service.

Kodiak:

Flirite, Inc.
Box 297
Kodiak AK 99615

Charter floats, wheels, or skis available for flightseeing tours or sport
fishing trips.

Island Air Service
Box 14
Kodiak AK 99615

Flightseeing tours of Kodiak Island
and Kodiak National Wildlife
Refuge. Flights to fishing streams.

Kodiak–Western Alaska
  Airlines
Box 2457
Kodiak AK 99615

This airline has amphibious and
wheeled aircraft in Kodiak, King
Salmon and Dillingham.

Kotzebue:

Shellabarger Flying Service
Box 11
Kotzebue AK 99752

Year-round charter service using
fixed-wing aircraft. Service to all
parts of the Seward Peninsula.

Walker Air Service
Box 57
Kotzebue AK 99752

Charters for skiing, hunting and
river floats. One to two weeks
notice.

McGrath:

Hub Air Service
Box 2
McGrath AK 99627

Charter service for flights to surrounding villages and sportfishing
locations.

Manley Hot Springs:

Hot Springs Aviation
Manley Hot Springs AK 99756

Contact Cyril D. Hetherington for
charters to surrounding mining area.

Naknek:

Griechen Air Taxi
Monte Handy
Box 161
Naknek AK 99633

Taxi service serving Bristol Bay and the Alaska Peninsula. Flights to the McNeil River State Bear Sanctuary, and fishing, hunting, and photo trips.

King Flying Service
Box 26
Naknek AK 99633

Sport hunting and sportfishing trips to Alaska Peninsula and Bristol Bay region.

Moose Pass:

Trail Lake Flying Service
Linda P. Flieger
Box 7
Moose Pass AK 99631

Wheel and float aircraft for fly-in to forest service cabins and hunting and fishing locations. Serving Kenai Peninsula and Prince William Sound.

Nome:

Bering Air, Inc.
Box 1650
Nome AK 99762

Charter service that also has flights to all of western Alaska on per-seat basis. Specialty flights and freight.

Foster Aviation
Box 1028
Nome AK 99762

Mail service to Point Clarence and Little Diomede Island, and air taxi service on Seward Peninsula.

Muntz Northern Airlines
Box 790
Nome AK 99762

Scheduled year-round service to Kotzebue, Seward Peninsula and arctic Alaska. Offices in Nome and Kotzebue.

Northway:

Northway Air Service
Box 410
Northway AK 99764

Charter services to surrounding area. Flightseeing, sportfishing, and photography.

Palmer:

Air Valley
Box 157
Palmer AK 99645

Matanuska Valley flightseeing tours and tours to Knik Glacier. State-wide air charter service.

Alaskan Airventures
Star Route C, Box 8762
Palmer AK 99645

Located on Snowshoe Lake at mile
148, Glenn Highway. Sportfishing
tours to area lakes.

Petersburg:

Alaska Island Air, Inc.
Box 508
Petersburg AK 99833

Glacier tours of LeConte Glacier
and charters for sportfishing and
sport hunting.

Sand Point:

Sand Point Air Service
Box 4
Sand Point AK 99661

Serving the Alaska Peninsula and
Aleutian Island chain. Direct
flights from Anchorage.

Seward:

Harbor Air Service
Box 1417
Seward AK 99664

Flightseeing in Kenai Fjords, Glacier
Bay, Harding Ice Field, and
Seward's sea lion rookeries.

Sitka:

Bellair
P.O. Box 371
Sitka AK 99835

Hunting and fishing trips and service to outlying towns and camps.
Charters anywhere in Southeast.

Mountain Aviation
P.O. Box 875
Sitka AK 99835

Based at Sitka Airport, this charter
service flies anywhere in Southeast.
Sportfishing and hunting locations.

Raven Copters
Box 2242
Sitka AK 99835

Photo trips by helicopter of Baranof
Island Glacier, Sitka Sound and Mt.
Edgecumbe.

Skagway:

Skagway Air Service
Ben Lingle
Box 357
Skagway AK 99840

Scenic flights over Chilkoot Trail
and White Pass. Also air tours of
Glacier Bay. Charters of Whitehorse, Haines, and Juneau.

Soldotna:

Dick's Flying Service
Box 1480
Soldotna AK 99669

Air tours of the Kenai Peninsula. Fly-in sportfishing, clam digging, and photography.

Talkeetna:

Hudson Air Service
Cliff Hudson
Talkeetna AK 99676

Glacier landings, expedition support, scenic flights, air supply to Mt. McKinley, statewide charters.

K-2 Aviation
Box 290
Talkeetna AK 99676

Specializes in air support for Mt. McKinley and Alaska Range climbers. Statewide charters, scenic flights.

Talkeetna Air Taxi
Doug Geeting
Box 73
Talkeetna AK 99676

Glacier landings, expedition support, sportfishing, sport hunting, aerial photography. Specialty is air supply to expeditions on Mt. McKinley.

Willow:

B & C Airventures
Buck Stewart
Box 1007
Willow AK 99688

Charter service for flightseeing tours, camping, waterfowl hunting, sportfishing, wildlife and scenic excursions around the state.

North Star Aviation
Box 1009
Willow AK 99688

Headquarters at 5000-foot airstrip with fuel for all types of aircraft. Flightseeing tours.

Willow Air Service
Box 42
Willow AK 99688

Sportfishing, wilderness camping, and photo tours at remote lake locations by floatplane.

Wrangell:

Stikine Air Service
Box 631
Wrangell AK 99929

Flightseeing over the Stikine River, glacier viewing over the Stikine Ice Field, and fly-in sportfishing.

Wrangell Mountains:

Howard's Flying Service
Box 31
Chitina AK 99566

Flights to McCarthy Lodge, Tonsina Glacier, Mt. Blackburn, and the old Kennicott Copper Mine.

Yakutat:

Gulf Air Taxi
Box 367
Yakutat AK 99689

Flights to many forest service cabins for sportfishing and hunting. Also flights to Malaspina Glacier.

Shipping Lines

There are many truck and moving van lines that serve Alaska from the lower forty-eight states. Some of these lines provide service overland through Canada, but most go overland to Seattle and then move goods via ship or barge to their destination. The following is a list of interstate ship and barge line services from Seattle to Alaska. Check with the shipping line to determine whether a particular destination is accessible year-round.

Alaska Marine Lines
7100 2nd Ave., S.W.
Seattle WA 98106

Boyer Alaska Barge Lines, Inc.
7318 4th Ave. South
Seattle WA 98108

Bureau of Indian Affairs
4735 E. Marginal Way South
Seattle WA 98134

Coastal Alaska Lines, Inc.
1031 W. Ewing Street
Seattle WA 98119

Crowley Maritime Corp.
4th and Battery Building
Seattle WA 98111

Foss Alaska Lines, Inc.
Terminal 115, P.O. Box 80587
Seattle WA 98108

Northland Services, Inc.
6425 N.E. 175th Street
Seattle WA 98155

Pacific Western Lines, Inc.
5225 E. Marginal Way South
Seattle WA 98134

Samson Tug and Barge, Inc.
337 N.W. 40th Street
Seattle WA 98107

Sea-Land Service, Inc.
2805 26th Avenue S.W.
Seattle WA 98114

Totem Ocean Trailer Express, Inc.
130 Sitcum Waterway, Alaska Terminal
Tacoma WA 98421

4. Land Ownership and Disposal

Of all the vast area which makes up Alaska's forests, valleys, mountain ranges, tundra, and rivers (375 million acres in all), only 160,000 acres show any sign of having been cleared, settled, or otherwise used by man. Two-thirds of Alaska's population remains clustered around two major population centers; over one half in the Anchorage bowl and surrounding areas accessible by highway. Long periods of dark and extreme cold play their part in the lack of settlement, as do the glaciers, mountains, rivers, and oceans, by presenting effective barriers to trade and commerce. One of the major limitations to land development was the fact that for the century prior to statehood, Alaska was in the hands of a single landowner — the United States government. In recent years, patterns of land ownership have been constantly changing. Land selection by three major contenders has been fast and furious and will continue so for some time to come. The three main contenders for land in Alaska are the federal government, the state of Alaska, and the natives.

From the time the United States purchased Alaska from Russia until the Alaska Statehood Act, Alaskan land was almost all federally owned. It was open to homesteading and other forms of private acquisition, but less than one half of one percent actually passed into private hands. At statehood, the federal government agreed to let the new state select 104 million acres out of the 375 million acres total as state land. In addition, the state was given title to submerged lands under navigable waterways as determined by the Submerged Lands Act.

Then Alaska's natives, whose claim to the state was recognized by Congress in 1884 but remained unsettled at statehood, relinquished their claim on December 18, 1971, with the passage of the Alaska Native Claims Settlement Act. This act of Congress was prompted by the fact that the north slope oil strike required a pipeline, and the resolution of native land claims was needed for a pipeline permit. The natives relinquished their claim to Alaska in return for nearly one billion dollars, the right to select 44 million acres from a land pool of some 116 million acres, and 2 million acres of water. Native lands and monies are now being administered by Alaska native village and regional corporations.

53

*Distinctive old two-story barns like the one above were built from govern-
ment plans handed out to the settlers who came to Alaska from the
Midwest. There was only one plan, so the barns are all alike.*

As soon as the Native Settlement Act had passed, the state requested
title to 77 million acres of land, to be selected before the native
withdrawals and before the federal government withdrew land for study
as national interest lands. The United States Department of the Interior
refused to recognize this selection by the state but in 1972, after litigation,
affirmed state selection of 41 million acres.

Since 1978 the federal government has designated 56 million acres of
Alaska as national monuments and created 106 million acres of new conservation units. Land selection by all parties is accelerating and by 1994,
when it is hoped that the land selection process will be complete, Alaska
will have been divided in the following manner:

- 110 million acres of land and water to the state
- 46 million acres of land and water to the natives
- 1.2 million acres to individual natives under a 1906 Native Allot-
  ment Act that gives each native the right to claim up to 160
  acres
- 1.35 million acres sold or homesteaded into private hands
- 52 million acres in national parks
- 77 million acres in national wildlife refuges

- 23 million acres in national forests
- 2.1 million acres in military reservations
- 65.7 million acres to be held as BLM land

Skirmishing on specific land-use conflicts will probably continue for years. For instance, there are pockets of native, state, and privately owned land within national park boundaries, and recently natives have proposed building a ten-story resort hotel on land they hold in the middle of Lake Clark National Park and Preserve. Similarly, there are mining claims and traditional subsistence hunting areas within national parks. Borax hopes to develop what may be the world's largest molybdenum deposit at Quartz Hill, a peak deep within Misty Fjords National Monument. Providing special hunting and fishing allowances for native and white subsistence hunters is a hot issue and one that has not yet been adequately resolved.

Acquiring private ownership of land in Alaska is done most easily by purchasing it from other private owners. Most privately owned land is located within cities and towns and along highways and access roads in the southcentral region and east and east-central interior. The major drawback to acquiring land in this manner is that it is in relatively short supply and not many large tracts are available. Speculation and land claim conflicts have made even small tracts of available land very expensive. There are also land settlement programs, in effect by both the federal and state governments, by which private land can be acquired.

Federal Land Disposal

Federal land disposal is currently limited to two remote areas. The first is about 240 air miles northwest of Anchorage near Lake Minchumina. The area has no road access. General access is by plane to Minchumina, then overland on foot. It is possible to reach the area from the north by riverboat along the Kantishna River or by floatplane to Wein Lake, which is about twenty air miles to the northeast. The land is open and rolling ranging from 600 feet elevation to over 4000 feet. Much of it is around the 1000-foot level. It is bisected by small north-flowing rivers and streams which flow out of the Sischu Mountains. The drainage includes tributary streams centering on the Lost River. Much of the land is also wooded, but the timber is scattered and is not readily available for house logs, nor is it of any commercial value. Temperature extremes range from eighty-nine degrees to a low of sixty-two degrees below zero. Average precipitation is thirteen to twenty inches and average snowfall is fifty-seven inches. Water quality is unknown. Much of the area is marshy with poor soils underlain with permafrost. The settlement area does not lie within any organized unit of local government, so there are no schools, post offices, commercial facilities, or utilities. The nearest emergency medical facilities are located in Fairbanks and Anchorage. In the two years that this 20,000-acre parcel has been open to settlement, only forty-five people have put in claims.

The second area open to settlement by the federal government became available in September of 1983 and is in an area of somewhat easier access—near Slana in southcentral Alaska. The Slana parcels encompass approximately 10,250 acres, about twenty-five miles northeast of Glennallen off the Glenn Highway near the junction of the Tok cutoff and Nabesna Road. The most common method of access is by automobile to Slana and then to the parcels via boat and all-terrain vehicle. There are also airstrips at Slana, Chistochina, and Tok. Nearby rivers are the Slana and Chistochina. The seasonal temperature ranges in the area are average summer temperatures of thirty-nine and sixty-nine degrees and winter averages of twelve below zero degrees to thirty-six degrees. Extremes range from minus fifty-one to ninety-three degrees. Average precipitation in the area is ten inches annually, which includes seventy-four inches of snow (seventy-four inches is equivalent to 5.25 inches of moisture). The terrain varies from mountain slopes above treeline, to low, rolling moraines, to flat lowlands. The vegetation also varies, with alpine tundra in the higher regions, spruce and hardwood forests in some upland and lowland sections, some areas of low brush and muskeg bog, and some areas of poplar forest. The surface water quality is unacceptable due to high silt loads on most of the area's glacially fed streams, particularly in summer. Surface waters in the lowlands may also contain objectionable amounts of iron and organic materials and so must be treated for use, but timber for house logs and firewood are readily available. Most residents of bush areas live a subsistence lifestyle, but many also have retirement or seasonal incomes to supplement subsistence hunting and trapping.

Under the federal program, land can be claimed in both the Minchumina and Slana settlement areas for the following three uses:

Homesite: A person can claim up to five acres as a homesite for $2.50 per acre if he resides on the property for a period of five months each year for three years during a five-year period and builds a habitable house on the property.

Headquarters Site: A person can claim up to five acres to be used as a headquarters to conduct a productive business of his own or that of his employer. The applicant has five years to prove that he is operating a productive business and then must bear the cost of surveying the land and pay a purchase price of $2.50 per acre. This type of claim is most often used for big-game guiding and trapping operations.

Trade and Manufacturing Site: An applicant can claim up to eighty acres for the operation of a business involving trade, manufacturing, or other productive industry. He has five years to prove his business and apply to purchase the land at $2.50 per acre. This type of site can be used for such things as roadhouses, handcrafted items for sale, lodges, recreation cabins, etc.

An applicant must be a U.S. citizen twenty-one years of age or older. Each applicant can receive title to only one homesite, one headquarter site, and one trade and manufacturing site. For a packet of information on federal settlement in Alaska write to:

Bureau of Land Management
Anchorage District Office
4700 E. 72nd Avenue
Anchorage AK 99507
Phone: (907) 267-1200

State Land Disposal

The state of Alaska has several land disposal programs by which private citizens can acquire state land. Applicants for all programs must be at least eighteen years old and must meet a residency requirement of one year for all but the auction program. The parcels offered are in various locations statewide. They are described in the state land disposal brochure, put out by the Department of Natural Resources Division of Land and Water Management. Full information describing parcels currently available under each program, date deadlines, procedures for filing, and applications can be obtained by sending $3.00 to one of the offices listed below.

Northcentral District
4420 Airport Way
Fairbanks AK 99701

Southcentral District
3601 C Street, Pouch 7-005
Anchorage AK 99510

Southeastern District
Marine View Apts., #407
230 South Franklin
Juneau AK 99801

Disposals usually occur each spring and fall. Successful applicants are determined by lottery if more than one qualified applicant has applied for a single parcel. Programs currently being used for disposal of state land are as follows:

Auction Program: This is the only state program that does not require residency. Selected parcels are sold at auction to the highest bidder and require a minimum bid of fair market value. Depending on the parcel the state may sell surface rights, lease surface or subsurface rights, or sell by restricted title.

Homesites: This program allows a resident of at least one year to obtain a homesite of five acres or less for the cost of the survey and platting. The person must build a permanent single-family dwelling on the property within five years and must live on the property for thirty-five months within seven years.

Lottery: A resident of at least one year may participate in the lottery program. A person may apply to purchase a homesite, subdivision parcel, or agricultural parcel. If he is the lottery winner on that particular parcel, he may buy the parcel at appraised value. A lottery applicant must be present at the drawing to win and must make a five percent down payment when his name is drawn. He may pay the balance in either quarterly or annual installments for a period of up to twenty years using the level payment concept. The interest rate is based on the prevailing rate for real estate mortgage loans made by the Federal Land Bank of Alaska, which varies from month to month. There is no prepayment penalty.

Homestead: In July of 1983 the legislature passed a bill which reinstated homesteading as a means of acquiring Alaskan land. The homestead law became effective July 1, 1984, and the first parcels of approximately 15,000 to 20,000 acres were offered through a lottery in the fall of 1984. Under the provisions of the homesteading law, a successful applicant may claim up to 40 acres of nonagricultural or up to 160 acres of agricultural land. The homesteader must stake the corners of the land and flag the boundaries. He must then file a description of the land with the state and pay a filing fee of $5.00 per acre. After filing, there are two different ways in which he can claim title to the property:

(1) The land may be purchased at fair market value after it has been staked, brushed and surveyed.
(2) The land is free if certain requirements are met. The homesteader must brush the boundaries within ninety days,

must complete an approved survey of the land within two years, must erect a permanent dwelling on the homestead within three years, and must live on the parcel for twenty-five months within five years. If the land is classified as agricultural, the homesteader must also clear and either put into production or prepare for cultivation twenty-five percent of the land within five years.

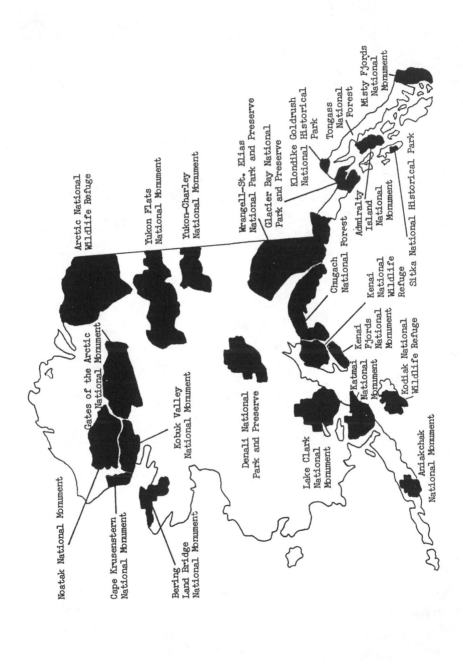

5. Alaska's National Parklands

Alaska's national forests, parks, preserves, refuges, and monuments are designed to preserve some of the most striking and unusual geological, archaeological, and historical features in North America, and at the same time to leave wildlife undisturbed. The most developed and best known of the forests and parks have designated trails, camping facilities, and road access and are visited by thousands of people each year. Many of the lesser-known parklands are accessible only by plane or boat and remain as they have been for centuries – untouched wilderness.

The two largest national forests in America, the Tongass and the Chugach, are found in southeast and southcentral Alaska. The wildlife refuges in various parts of the state are designed to protect some of the most rare and unusual animals on the North American Continent, including the Kodiak brown bear, the porcupine caribou herd, and the endangered peregrine falcon. In national parks and monuments are hauntingly beautiful geologic formations, such as the granite cliffs, bays, and coves in Misty Fjords National Monument, or the volcanic Valley of 10,000 Smokes at Katmai. Nature's forces carving new landscapes can be witnessed at the ever-changing Glacier Bay National Park and Preserve near Haines.

Alaska is the one remaining state in which land is still being designated by Congress as national parks, forests, wildlife refuges, wild and scenic areas, or national interest lands. Boundaries of existing parks are still subject to change, and it will be a matter of years before the final status of all federal lands is determined.

Opposite: *Alaska's natural forests, parks, preserves, refuges, and monuments.*

National Park Service Lands

Aniakchak National Monument and Preserve

Located on the Alaska Peninsula 400 miles southwest of Anchorage, this monument boasts one of the largest volcanic craters in the world, nearly six miles wide and 2000 feet deep. The park encompasses 514,000 acres, and camping is permitted, although there are no designated areas or facilities. Overnight facilities are available in King Salmon, 150 miles from the park. Air charters from King Salmon or from Port Heiden, ten miles west of the monument, provide transportation to and from the park.

Bering Land Bridge National Preserve

Located on the Seward Peninsula between Nome and Kotzebue, this is the spot which is believed to have been the land route used by the first inhabitants of North America. Most of the route now lies underwater. Hundreds of clear lakes, streams, and lagoons provide excellent sport fishing locations for salmon, char, grayling, and pike. Wildlife in the 2,457,000-acre preserve includes seals, whales, grizzly bears, wolves, and moose. Camping is permitted, but there are no developed facilities, so campers must be self-sufficient. Charters to the preserve are available from Nome and Kotzebue.

Cape Krusenstern National Monument

This 560,000-acre monument borders the Chukchi Sea and Kotzebue Sound in Alaska's far north. It is archeologically important because of layers of artifacts found in the soil, which reveal successive phases of native development over the centuries. The monument is known for backpacking and camping, although there are no developed facilities. Charter flights to the monument are available from Kotzebue, ten miles to the southeast.

Denali National Park and Preserve

In the Athabascan Indian language Denali means "great one," an appropriate name for the park which has 20,320-foot Mt. McKinley as its focal point. This is the best known and most popular of all wilderness

View of North America's tallest peak, Mt. McKinley, from milepost 135.2 of the George Parks Highway. Called Denali–"the great one"–by the Indians, this mighty mountain can be seen from Anchorage nearly 150 miles away on a clear day.

recreation areas in Alaska. It is served both by highway and by the Alaskan Railroad. Rental cars are available at the park, and free shuttle bus services are administered by the park service for transportation within the park. There are several hotels, inns, and lodges nearby, as well as a park hotel within the boundaries. There are seven campgrounds with a total of 228 camping spaces. The many things to see and do within Denali National Park include guided hikes, tundra wildlife tours, raft trips in Nenana River Canyon, horse trail rides, flightseeing tours, and in winter, cross-country skiing and guided sled dog tours. Denali National Park and Preserve is one of the best places in Alaska for viewing wildlife, which includes barren ground caribou, grizzly bears, Dall sheep, and more than 150 species of birds.

Gates of the Arctic National Park and Preserve

Located in the central Brooks Range, this national park's 7,952,000 acres reach from the southern foothills to the north slope. The long mountain valleys are ideal for hiking, camping and fishing, and the rivers and creeks make great places to raft, canoe or kayak. The park is also very popular with mountain climbers. There are no established trails or facilities within the park, but guides and outfitters are available in Fairbanks. Wildlife includes caribou, Dall sheep, and grizzly bears. Access to the park is by air charter from Fairbanks to Bettles or to Anaktuvuk Pass. Charters are also available from Bettles. It is now possible to drive the Dalton Highway as far as Disaster Creek near Dietrich Camp. This point is close to the boundary of Gates of the Arctic, but there are no roads other than the highway, and no one without a permit is allowed to continue past Disaster Creek.

Glacier Bay National Park and Preserve

Located just 60 miles north of Juneau, this ice-age park has been called one of the seven natural wonders of the world. Frozen rivers of ice spill out of awesome mountains and calve giant icebergs into the sea, thus forming the largest concentration of tidewater glaciers in the world. Whales romp in the icy waters, and seals can often be seen basking on ice floes. A variety of tours are available to view the magnificent scenery, including cruiseboat tours, seaplane tours, and guided kayak tours. Glacier Bay Lodge on Bartlett Cove is the center for visitor facilities at Glacier Bay.

Katmai National Monument and Preserve

Katmai is located in the Aleutian Range on the Alaska Peninsula, 290 miles southwest of Anchorage. It is a one-of-a-kind place, where glacial ice and volcanic fire meet in a wilderness park containing 2,800,000 acres. Within Katmai is the Valley of 10,000 Smokes, formed in 1912 when Mt. Novarupta exploded and left in its wake an ash-filled valley where steam rose from countless fumaroles. Some of these smoking holes can still be seen. The landscape in Katmai is still dynamic, and major changes could occur at any time if the volcanoes of Katmai should erupt. The many dormant and active volcanoes of the Aleutian Range and the many island-studded lakes fringed with thick forests make Katmai National Monument an ideal place to study and explore unspoiled nature. The alpine streams, braided rivers, and a coastline of fjords, bays, and beaches are wonderful places to camp and fish. Many tours are available to and within the monument, and facilities within the park include Lake Grosvenor Camp and the Brooks River Lodge on Naknek Lake. Both have dining facilities and cabins.

Kenai Fjords National Monument

This 567,000-acre park is located along the gulf coast of the eastern Kenai Peninsula. It includes a wilderness of glacier-carved mountain valleys and fjords, several tidewater glaciers, and the 300-square-mile Harding Ice Field that buries all but the peaks of the central Kenai Mountains. No campgrounds exist within the monument, but many cruise and guide services are available in nearby Homer and Seldovia. Some of these guides provide accommodations in their camps. Fishing and swimming, glacier hiking, beach cookouts, and boating around the fjords are popular activities.

Klondike Goldrush National Historical Park

The Klondike Goldrush National Historical Park is more than just a place—it is the spirit of thousands of frenzied men and women rushing to the gold fields in the Klondike. Visitors to the park will travel in the footsteps of the stampeders. The United States National Park Service and Parks Canada have cooperated in researching and planning the park, as part of it lies in Canada. Park experiences range from urban to small-town to wilderness as one follows the trail from Skagway to the Chilkoot and White passes to the historic town of Dawson. Museums along the route tell the Klondike story. Restored riverboats at Carcross, Whitehorse, and Dawson tell the paddlewheeler chapter of the Klondike's history. The thirty-three-mile Chilkoot Trail is accessible only on foot and is the most challenging way to follow the route to the Yukon's headwaters. It is a difficult hike and usually takes four days. A less strenuous method of following the overland route is to go by automobile via the Skagway-Carcross road over White Pass, with special turnouts at White Pass City and the infamous Dead Horse Gulch. The narrow-gauge White Pass and Yukon Railroad, which formerly ran daily between Whitehorse and Bennett, closed down in 1982, but it is hoped that service will be restored in the not-too-distant future. The railroad affords a spectacular view of the gold rush route through White Pass as it winds through canyons and over mountain passes on one of the steepest railroad grades in North America.

Kobuk Valley National Park

Sandwiched between the Waring and Baird Mountains is the 1,710,000-acre Kobuk Valley National Park, which contains the great

Kobuk Sand Dunes. The dunes originated from glacial silt and cover a 350-square-mile area. The park also contains boreal forests of open woodland underlain by thick tundra. Main access to the park is from Kotzebue, seventy-five miles to the west, where flights can be chartered to Kiana or Ambler. From these small villages, most people then backpack into the park. There are no established trails, facilities, or services in Kobuk Valley National Park.

Lake Clark National Park and Preserve

About 100 miles southwest of Anchorage, across Cook Inlet from the Kenai Peninsula, the Alaskan and Aleutian mountain ranges converge in the 5,653,000-acre Lake Clark National Park and Preserve. The area boasts steaming volcanoes, rugged mountains, craggy peaks, alpine valleys, blue-green glaciers, free-flowing rivers, and sparkling lakes. Predominantly wilderness in character, the park particularly appeals to hikers, backpackers, and climbers seeking relatively low but challenging mountains. Wildlife within the park includes black, brown and grizzly bears, Dall sheep, moose, caribou, wolves, and lynx. Birds include bald eagles and hawks, waterfowl, and many kinds of seabirds. There are grayling, northern pike, trout, and salmon for the sport fisherman. Several lodges located along Lake Clark offer accommodations and services within the park. These services include making arrangements and supplying equipment for backpackers, cross-country skiers, and those planning float trips. Access to Lake Clark National Park and Preserve is by air charter from Anchorage, Kenai, or Homer.

Noatak National Monument and Preserve

The Noatak National Monument and Preserve is the largest mountain-ringed watershed in North America and contains 6,460,000 acres. The Noatak River flows through a broad valley nearly 150 miles long that serves as a natural highway. Great herds of caribou cross the river during seasonal migrations to and from their calving grounds. The boreal forest gives way to treeless tundra in the valley, and canoeing, rafting, kayaking, and backpacking are popular activities. The monument is located about sixty miles from Kotzebue; access is by charter flight from Kotzebue or Bettles, where outfitters will fly in boats and passengers. There are no maintained trails, facilities, or services within the monument.

Sitka National Historical Park

This 100-acre park is located on southeast Alaska's Baranof Island within walking distance of the city of Sitka. It is the site of a historic Tlingit Indian fort where, in 1804, Russian troops under Alexander Baranof defeated the Indians in a battle that marked the end of Indian resistance to the coming of foreigners to their shores. Today some eighteen totem poles stand near the visitor center and on the nearly two miles of forested trails that wind through the park. Picnic tables and shelters are conveniently located along the trails.

Wrangell–St. Elias National Park and Preserve

The largest national park in the United States, the Wrangell–St. Elias occupies 12,318,000 acres in southcentral Alaska. Bordering the Yukon Territory and Canada's Kluane National Park on the east, the Wrangell–St. Elias extends from the Tetlin lowlands in the north, through the high mountains of the Wrangell and St. Elias chains, to the coastal beaches of the Gulf of Alaska. The broad Chitina River Valley, the Malaspina Glacier, and the Icy and Yakutat bays are included in this area. The park contains some of the highest mountains in North America including the third highest, Mt. St. Elias, which is 18,008 feet tall. Opportunities for wilderness backpacking, lake fishing, car camping, river running, cross-country skiing, and mountain climbing abound. There is road access into the park from the community of Chitina via the Chitina-McCarthy road, which extends sixty-five miles up the Chitina River Valley to the town of McCarthy. There is also a road from Slana on the Tok cutoff that extends into the park some forty-five miles to the abandoned mining community of Nabesna. All other access is by air. Charter aircraft are available in most Alaskan cities, including Cordova, Valdez, Glennallen, and McCarthy. Rustic overnight accommodations are available in McCarthy. Excursions to the abandoned Kennecott Copper Mine six miles from McCarthy are popular with visitors.

Yukon-Charley Rivers National Preserve

Deep within interior Alaska, the Yukon and Charley rivers bring together natural and human history in this 1,713,000-acre preserve, the home of the peregrine falcon. During the long winter, the preserve lies locked in ice, cold, and darkness, and the few that will visit it then must be expedition-equipped. Summer weather is also extreme. Daytime temperatures as high as ninety degrees may be followed by freezing nights, and frontal storms may cause day after day of rain. Biting insects abound. Summer travel depends mainly on the rivers. Most popular is the float trip down the Yukon, with side explorations up major tributaries and day hikes in bordering highlands. Rafts and canoes allow the greatest flexibility. Yukon-Charley is a vast and sometimes hostile environment with no parkland facilities. The small staff can provide only minimal patrol or rescue services. You must assume you are completely on your own once you leave the well-traveled Yukon corridor. Access to the park is from Eagle, at the preserve's upriver end, and from Circle at its lower end. Overnight accommodations and basic groceries and supplies are available in both cities.

U.S. Forest Service Lands

Admiralty Island National Monument

The 900,000-acre Admiralty Island National Monument includes most of Admiralty Island, the largest island in Southeast Alaska. Parts of the island lie only twelve miles from Juneau, but even so, it is considered to be an ideal wilderness laboratory for studying wildlife and plants in their natural habitat. There are more brown bears on this island than there are people, and the largest concentration of nesting bald eagles in North America resides here. The largest settlement is Angoon, a village of about 550 Tlingit Indians who still depend on the forest and ocean for their subsistence. There are fifteen public-use cabins scattered throughout the monument, maintained by the Forest Service. Access to Angoon is by air from Juneau or by ferry on the Marine Highway System.

Chugach National Forest

Located in southcentral Alaska just southeast of Anchorage, the Chugach National Forest occupies most of Prince William Sound, the northeastern third of the Kenai Peninsula, and the Copper River Delta. It is the second largest national forest in America. On the edges of Prince William Sound the forests are mostly of Sitka spruce and western hemlock, while on the Kenai Peninsula there are thousands of acres of birch, aspen, white spruce, and spindly black spruce. There are numerous highway-accessible campgrounds and picnic areas amid the lakes, rivers, and mountains in the forest. There are many small remote access cabins maintained by the Forest Service. There are over 100 miles of designated trails for hiking, and tranquil alpine lakes, winding fjords, and hidden coves for boaters or anglers. Portage and Columbia glaciers are popular attractions in the area.

Misty Fjords National Monument

Some of the southeast Alaska's most magnificent scenery lies within this 3,570-square-mile national monument near Ketchikan. Sheer granite cliffs rise to 3000 feet above the deep narrow inlet of the Pacific Ocean that winds into the monument. Lush forests of Sitka spruce, western hemlock, and cedar cling to the steep walls of the fjords, and in the mountain valleys the alpine meadows are covered with wildflowers. Three major rivers and hundreds of small streams are located within the monument. Mineral springs, lava flows, and deposits of gold, silver, and copper can also be found. Access to the monument is by floatplane or boat. Tours are available from Ketchikan.

The Tongass National Forest

The Tongass National Forest is the largest national forest in America and includes nearly all of southeast Alaska, stretching from Ketchikan on the south to Skagway and Yakutat on the north. It contains 16 million acres, is 500 miles long and up to 100 miles wide. Within the Tongass there are more than 130 public recreation cabins and five wilderness study areas. Recreation within the Tongass National Forest includes nearly everything that southeast Alaska has to offer: fishing, hunting, skiing, boating, hiking, camping, prospecting, and guided tours. Most of the cities of the Tongass are ports of call on the Alaska Marine Highway System. Rain is common in Southeast, so raingear must be included for outdoor sports.

U.S. Fish and Wildlife Service Lands

Arctic National Wildlife Range

Located in the extreme northeast corner of Alaska, this 18,054,624-acre refuge is the home of the porcupine caribou herd, which numbers about 120,000 animals. People who have seen the herd from the air say that it sometime stretches for as much as ten miles and is nearly a mile wide. Other wildlife in the range includes moose, bears, wolverines, wolves, lynx, Dall sheep, foxes, martens, otters, and falcons.

Kenai National Wildlife Refuge

More than 9000 moose live in this 1,970,000-acre refuge located on the northwest Kenai Peninsula. The refuge is also home to Dall sheep, brown and black bears, and mountain goats, who use the refuge as kidding grounds.

Kodiak National Wildlife Refuge

This 1,900,000-acre refuge is located on the southwestern two-thirds of Kodiak Island. The refuge is world famous for its population of Kodiak brown bears. Other wildlife within the refuge are Dall sheep, moose, reindeer, mountain goats, deer, and elk. The refuge is also noted for the many salmon that spawn in the island's streams.

Alaska State Parks

There are presently eighty-three state parks, state historical parks, state recreation areas, and waysides administered by the state of Alaska. All facilities in the Alaska State Park System are on a first-come, first-served basis, and reservations are not presently needed for any facilities. Information concerning lawful hunting in state parks may be obtained from the Division of Parks offices or the Department of Fish and Game, although firearms are not to be used in waysides or campgrounds. Described below are some of the larger and better known of the state parks, but information on all areas can be obtained by writing to the addresses listed in the address section.

Chilkat State Park

Located south of Haines on the Chilkat Peninsula, Chilkat State Park is the place to go to spot eagles, fish for salmon, glimpse glaciers, comb the beaches, and enjoy the beauty of the rugged mountains and maritime forests of southeast Alaska. The park includes a campground, trails, a boat ramp, and picnic areas. Hiking and boating are popular activities in the summer, while cross-country skiing is the winter activity of choice.

Chugach State Park

This park is located right in the backyard of Anchorage. There are plenty of places to picnic, climb, kayak, hike, ski, snowmobile, fish, or pick berries. You can camp in a developed campground or in a secluded backcountry valley. You can float a river or photograph wildflowers by an isolated glacial tarn. Wildlife viewing and spectacular scenery are available year-round on established trails and routes throughout the park. Several descriptive brochures are available on request.

Denali State Park

Located in the spectacular country of the Alaska Range about 130 miles north of Anchorage, Denali State Park offers excellent views of Mt. McKinley. There are major campgrounds and a growing trail system within the boundaries. Brochures are available.

Katchemak Bay State Park and State Wilderness Park

Both parks offer wild mountainous terrain and ocean shoreline rich in scenery and wildlife. Located on the southwest tip of the Kenai Peninsula, these undeveloped parks are reached by boat or plane, usually from Homer across the bay. Boating, fishing, and beachcombing are outstanding in the tree-lined coves, bays, and fjords highlighted by glaciers fed by the Harding Ice Field.

Wood-Tikchik State Park

The largest state park in the United States, Wood-Tikchik is an undeveloped wilderness park accessible by air from Dillingham. Located in western Alaska, it offers opportunities for fishing and boating in two separate systems of interconnected lakes. Because the park is surrounded by mountains to the west and tundra to the east, the variety and terrain offer superb sightseeing. Wilderness lodges on private parcels of land within the park boundaries offer food, shelter, transportation, and sport-fishing packages.

Chena River State Recreation Area

This is a large and presently undeveloped park which offers opportunities for fishing, swimming, primitive camping, and hunting. Winter activities such as snowmobiling, cross-country skiing and dogsledding are also possible in this recreation area. It is located on the Chena Hot Springs Road in the rolling hills east of Fairbanks.

Captain Cook State Recreation Area

Located north of Kenai, this recreation area is one of the few developed yet uncrowded parks where you can enjoy the lakes, rivers, forests, wildlife, and saltwater beaches of the Kenai Peninsula. Several drive-in and remote campgrounds and picnic areas are situated to take advantage of the wooded bluffs overlooking Cook Inlet and the sandy shores of Stormy Lake. There are trails to hike and ski, beaches to explore, waters to fish, and a place to launch your small boat. The Swanson River Canoe Trail terminates at a boat launch in the park.

Harding Lake State Recreation Area

This recreational area is a small but highly developed park on the Richardson Highway near Fairbanks. Harding Lake, with its tree-lined shores and sandy beaches, provides plenty of places to camp, picnic, fish, boat, and swim. Ice fishing, snowmobiling, and cross-country skiing are popular in the winter.

Nancy Lake State Recreation Area

Located just south of Willow on the George Parks Highway, Nancy Lake is an ideal place for canoeing, fishing, and boating on a network of more than 130 lakes and ponds, or for camping, hiking, and picnicking in the forests around these lakes. Winter brings out the skiers, snowshoers, snowmobilers, and dog-mushers. A nature trail, hiking and ski trails, and a system of canoe portages help you enjoy this park. Brochures are available.

The Chilkoot Trail

This is the most famous of the Klondike gold rush routes and offers a rugged thirty-three-mile hike through history and the backcountry terrain of southeast Alaska and British Columbia. The park is managed cooperatively with the National Park Service and Parks Canada. This difficult trail is not for everyone. The steep climb from the scales to the summit of the pass is extremely intimidating. Even if you are lucky enough to have good weather, the trail is long and strenuous. With weather at its worst, even experienced hikers will encounter difficulties. Exposure to wet, cold, and windy conditions combined with the exhausting climb to the summit is a major obstacle to all hikers. It is recommended that preparatory information be obtained from the U.S. National Park Service before attempting to hike the Chilkoot. The trail is not a wilderness hike. You will share the trail with many other hikers. The heaviest concentration of people occurs in July and August.

Baranof Castle Hill State Historic Park

Located in Sitka, this park is a scenic overview with interpretive plaques marking the site of the Russian-American governor's residence. It was here on October 18, 1867, that Alaska was transferred from Russia to the United States.

Old Sitka State Historic Park

Located on the beach north of Sitka, this state park commemorates the Russian establishment of Sitka and the resulting conflict with the native inhabitants. There is a scenic picnic area with historic markers.

Fort Abercrombie State Historic Park

Perched on a forested cliff northeast of Kodiak, this park is an ideal spot for coastal fortification. A major campground development is underway here, and plans to restore the World War II fort are progressing. While you camp, picnic, and explore the remains of the fort, remember that the Japanese actually did invade U.S. soil in Alaska.

Rika's Landing State Historic Park

This park celebrates the importance of roadhouses in the history of Alaska. From 1909 to 1947, Rika's Roadhouse was a key stop for travelers along the route now known as the Richardson Highway. Restoration is now underway.

6. Alaska's Cities

Southeastern Alaska

Haines

Haines is in southeast Alaska on the Chilkat Peninsula, ninety miles north of Juneau. Surrounded by mountains, it is near the end of the Alaska Marine Highway System and is one of three cities in Southeast that are connected by land to the rest of the state. The Haines Highway links the city to the Alaska Highway at Haines Junction, 157 miles north of Haines.

Haines' economy is based primarily on the wood products industry, fisheries, tourism, and crafts production. Though influenced by seasonal factors, the economy provides employment for nearly all residents on a year-round basis.

There are many things to see and do in Haines. Glacier Bay National Park lies only twelve minutes west of Haines, its closest neighbor. A variety of tours are available to view this largest concentration of tidewater glaciers in the world. Haines also boasts the largest gathering of bald eagles to be found anywhere in the world. The peak period is October through January, when literally thousands of eagles line the banks of the Chilkat River to feast on spawned-out salmon.

The famous Chilkat Dancers give performances in authentic Tlingit Indian costume several days a week at the Chilkat Center for the Performing Arts. Special events in Haines include the Haines King Salmon Derby in May, the Haines Fourth of July Celebration, the Southeast Alaska State Fair in August, and the Bald Eagle Bicentennial Celebration in June.

Limitless hiking trails, four state parks and recreation areas, superb fishing, and varied winter sports make Haines an exciting place to be at any time of the year.

The cities of the southeast.

Juneau

Juneau, Alaska's capital city, is located on the southeast coast of Alaska, 1,090 miles north of Seattle, Washington. Just off the beautiful Inside Passage, Juneau is surrounded by towering mountains and glaciers. Juneau is a charming city with narrow winding streets, many historic sites, and quaint residential areas. The city can be reached only by sea or air, but once there, cars can be rented for sightseeing on local roads. Within easy driving distance is Mendenhall Glacier, where float trips are available on the Mendenhall River. Glacier walks are also popular.

The largest winter recreation area in Southeast is Eaglecrest Ski Resort, with thirty runs, two chair lifts, and an ice skating rink. It is about thirty minutes from Juneau by car.

Charter boats are available to Tracy Arm, a glacier fed fjord south of Juneau, or to Skagway via Lynn Canal.

Most of the points of interest in the city of Juneau are within easy walking distance, and walking tour guides can be obtained at the Juneau Visitor Center.

Juneau has been the capital of Alaska since 1900, when the seat of government was transferred from Sitka. Although a site was chosen for a new capital in Southcentral, Alaskan voters rejected funding for the move in the 1982 elections and the capital remains in Juneau. The state legislature is in session for 150 days beginning in January. Government is the leading industry in Juneau, followed by trade and services.

Juneau is served by major airlines and by the Alaska Marine Highway System and is a port of call for nearly every cruise line that operates in Southeast.

Ketchikan

Ketchikan, a picturesque waterfront community built at the base of towering mountains, is the southernmost city in Southeast and is known for its lush forests, tingling rain-washed air, fishing, lumbering, and totemic arts. Situated on a narrow shelf of land on Revillagigedo Island, Ketchikan is the first stop for many travelers to Alaska. Its name comes from a Tlingit Indian word meaning "salmon creek," and fishing is the city's largest industry. One of the world's outstanding collection of totem poles is displayed in Ketchikan, along with many other examples of Tlingit, Tsimshian, and Haida Indian art.

Fishing, hunting, hiking, boating, and camping are popular recreational pursuits in the Ketchikan area. The National Forest Service maintains forty public-use cabins in the area for fly-in camping in a wilderness setting. There are also numerous other campsites nearby. Forty miles of local roads provide sightseeing ease, and boat and bus tours are also readily available.

Ketchikan is on major airline routes and is also served by the Marine Highway. Twenty-two miles to the east of Ketchikan is the hauntingly beautiful scenery of Misty Fjords National Monument with its spectacular sea cliffs and incredible natural splendor. Access to the monument is by either floatplane or charter boat. Package tours are available in Ketchikan.

Petersburg

Petersburg is located in southeast Alaska on Mitkof Island, midway between Juneau and Ketchikan. Famous as a fishing and logging center, Petersburg is known as Alaska's "Little Norway" since the majority of Petersburg residents are of Norwegian descent. Many of the houses are colorfully painted and the gardens carefully tended as is the custom among Scandinavians. Each year the people hold the Little Norway Festival on the weekend closest to May 17, Norway's independence day.

Fishing and sightseeing are two of the most popular activities for visitors to Petersburg. Charters for both saltwater and freshwater fishing are available locally, and visitors enjoy the tours conducted through the salmon cannery. Boat sightseeing tours of the area are worth the effort, as one of the most scenic portions of the Inside Passage lies between Petersburg and Wrangell in the Wrangell Narrows.

Jet flights serve Petersburg from Seattle and Anchorage, as well as from several other cities in Southeast. The Marine Highway ferries stop at Petersburg several times per week.

Sitka

Sitka is located in southeast Alaska on the west coast of Baranof Island on Sitka Sound. It is the only community in the Alexander Archipelago that fronts on the Pacific Ocean and is considered to be one of Alaska's most beautiful seacoast communities. Baranof Island is dotted with lakes, and the city lies beneath Mt. Edgecumbe, an extinct volcano often called the "Mt. Fuji" of the Western Hemisphere.

Sitka is a city rich in history. In 1741, the Russian landing near Sitka was the first landfall in Alaska by outsiders. Sitka became the capital city of Russian America and was romantically known as the Paris of the Pacific. Baranof's Castle, the only genuine castle in North America, was built in 1836. For a hundred years the castle's light was the only navigational aid on Alaska's entire coastline. Hundreds of ships from all nations of the world dropped anchor in Sitka Sound. The American flag first flew over Alaskan soil at Capital Hill in Sitka on October 18, 1867. Russian folkdances are still performed for visitors, and the Sheldon Jackson Museum contains artifacts from the Russian era.

Sitka is now the center for Alaska's wood products industry. Fishing and fish processing are also important industries, as is tourism, which contributes to the growth of the trade and service sectors.

Sightseeing tours are available in Sitka. Charter boats can be hired for sportfishing. Annual events include the Sitka Summer Music Festival during the first three weeks of June. With daily jet service and frequent ferry service, Sitka is a convenient stop for nearly everyone. It is also a port of call on Inside Passage cruises.

Skagway

Skagway is located at the northernmost point on the Inside Passage of southeast Alaska. The town is situated on a level area at the mouth of the Skagway River and is surrounded by mountains rising to 7000 feet. The name Skagway is said to mean "home of the north wind" in the local Tlingit Indian dialect. The city is about ninety miles north of Juneau.

Once a town approaching 10,000 people, the city of Skagway now has a permanent population of less than 1000. During the gold rush days nearly 50,000 persons poured into Skagway within two years and hiked the passes to Dawson in the Yukon. The Klondike Gold Rush National Historical Park is near Skagway, and many people, especially in the summer, still come to hike the rugged Chilkoot trail where artifacts of the gold rush days can still be seen.

The summers in Skagway are usually mild with an average temperature of fifty-seven degrees. Winters are brisk and invigorating, with temperatures frequently below freezing. The average annual precipitation is about twenty-nine inches.

Camping, hiking, fishing, and mountain climbing are popular recreational activities in Skagway, and there are many historical points of interest in and around the city.

Skagway is served by airlines and by the Alaska Marine Highway System. It is also one of three Southeast cities with highway connections to the Interior. Klondike Highway 2 connects Skagway to the Alaska Highway via Carcross and Whitehorse. The other two cities with highway connections are Haines and Hyder. Hyder is in the extreme southeast corner of the southeast region and is served by Canadian Highway 37A, a short access road to the Cassiar Highway 37, which connects Kitwanga near Prince Rupert with Watson Lake on the Alaska Highway in the Yukon Territory.

Wrangell

Wrangell is located near the mouth of the Stikine River, ninety miles north of Ketchikan. Situated on the northwest tip of Wrangell Island on Zimovia Strait, the city stretches up the slopes of wooded hillsides. It is the home of Alaska's logging industry and is the entry point to the historic Stikine River Country. The Stikine River was one of the major transportation routes for gold seekers during the Yukon gold rush in the late 1800s. It was also the route to many placer claims near Dease Lake in the 1870s. Guided rafting trips and charter flights for sightseeing on the river are available in Wrangell.

Ancient petroglyphs estimated to be over 8000 years old are visible along the beach in Wrangell at low tide. These rock carvings of birds and animals are a mystery whose origin is unknown.

Marine life near Wrangell most notably includes killer whales, seals, and migrating salmon. The river delta grasslands are habitat for moose and bear. There are large concentrations of eagles and ravens along the river and its tributaries. The immense delta flats are prime resting and feeding grounds for waterfowl, including snow geese and swans. Opportunities for fishing, hunting, hiking, and camping are abundant near Wrangell, and photographers will enjoy photographing the Stikine Ice Fields less than twenty minutes away by air.

Daily jet flights connect Wrangell to Seattle and Juneau, and commuter flights are available to other Southeast cities. The Marine Highway services the city several times a week.

Southcentral Alaska

Anchorage

The city of Anchorage is situated on the upper shores of Cook Inlet in southcentral Alaska, about 2484 miles northwest of Seattle, Washington. The Anchorage "bowl" is a flat alluvial plain flanked by the waters of Turnagain Arm to the south and Knik Arm to the north. The city lies within the V-shaped area created by these two bodies of water and is backed on the east by the Chugach Mountains, which range in height from 3000 to 5000 feet. The city sits on a bluff 114 feet above the water amid dense forests of spruce, birch, and aspen.

Even though Anchorage is a typical urban city and the hub of the southern road network, the edges of the wilderness are still only twenty minutes from downtown. It has been awhile since bears have been spotted walking down city streets, but moose are a common sight in Anchorage yards, especially in the suburbs during winter. Moose-vs.-auto accidents are frequent, particularly on the Glenn Highway in the northern suburbs. Residents of Anchorage still calculate the coming of winter by

The cities of the southcentral.

the first dusting of snow on the Chugach Mountains, called "termination dust."

Anchorage is a curious mixture of city sophistication and the informal frontier way of life. New modern hotels stand amid miles of trails that crisscross the city for bikers in summer and cross-country skiers in winter. Small log cabins and houses with neat flower gardens stand side by side with glass-enclosed hotels and high-rise office buildings. Elegant restaurants serve international cuisine alongside fast food places featuring

The Iditarod Trail Sled Dog Race is the big winter event in Alaska. In 1986, seventy-three "mushers" started out on the 1,049-mile trail from Anchorage to Nome. The race commemorates a time when dogsleds delivered a life-saving vaccine to the people of Nome, who were suffering a diphtheria outbreak. Top: Excitement mounts just prior to harnessing up for the big race. Bottom: Mushers start out every two minutes; teams line up for several blocks to await their turn.

Top: *Keystone Cops take the place of local police during the race, constantly searching for those "criminals" not wearing an Iditarod button.* Bottom: *Susan Butcher, who had hopes of being the first woman to win the Iditarod, had her hopes dashed in 1985 when a moose attacked her dog team. (Libby Riddles, not shown, became the first woman to win.) However, in 1986, Susan Butcher did win—and set an all-time record of 11 days, 15 hours, and 6 minutes.*

Kodiak burgers. Entertainment ranges from country and western music to the opera and ballet.

There are about forty hotels and motels in the Anchorage area. Some of the major hotel chains represented are the Hilton, Holiday Inn, and TraveLodge. The largest hotel is the Captain Cook Hotel with 600 rooms. The tallest is the twenty-two-story Anchorage Westward Hilton. Another large hotel is the Sheffield House, an Alaskan chain. Downtown rates average $70 to $100 for double accommodations, while other fine accommodations may be found further out for $45.

There are about 250 restaurants in Anchorage, including Japanese, Mexican, Chinese, Italian, and American. There are pizza parlors and delicious barbecue and seafood places, as well as numerous fast food chains.

The people of Anchorage value their recreational activities above almost everything else, and on weekends and holidays the city becomes an outdoor playground. During the summer the many parks and the miles of trails become havens for picnickers, joggers, bikers, tennis players, and swimmers. In winter there is sledding, skating, snowshoeing, hockey, skiing, dog-mushing, and swimming in one of several indoor pools. The Alyeska Ski Resort just south of Anchorage is open year-round and offers both winter and summer activities. At present it has five chair lifts, a ski lodge, rental condominiums, and lighted slopes for night skiing. Arctic Valley, located on military land within the city limits, is operated by a non-profit ski club. There are several other ski tows within the city limits operated by the city of Anchorage.

The Chugach State Park east of the city encompasses 495,000 acres of wilderness, with established trails for hiking, horseback riding, cross-country skiing, and snowmobiling.

A major annual event in Anchorage is the Anchorage Fur Rendezvous (called "Rondy"), held each February. The event began as a fur auction attracting buyers from around the world and now includes arts and crafts exhibits, a miners' and trappers' ball, a blanket toss, and dog-mushing competition which determines the world champion dogs for racing and weight pulling.

Cordova

Cordova is located on the shores of Orca Inlet between the Gulf of Alaska and Prince William Sound. It is about 1350 air miles northwest of Seattle, Washington.

Nestled in a panorama of greenery, mountains, water, and sky, the Cordova area strikes many travelers and settlers as the most scenic of

Alaska. The city came into being when the Northwestern Copper River Railroad was built in the early 1900s to bring the rich copper ore from the Kennicott Mines in the Copper Valley to an ocean port. Fishing has taken up where the railroad left off. Cordova is now a small fishing community that has virtually all the conveniences of any large metropolitan center while at the same time retaining its frontier way of life.

Marine life in Cordova includes sockeye, king, pink, and silver salmon, crabs, and razor, butter, and pink-neck clams. Wildlife and waterfowl that can be found within a few minutes of the city include moose, brown bear, deer, goats, ducks, eagles, geese, and the rare Canada dusky goose. Numerous lakes and streams in the Cordova area provide many kinds of freshwater fish for the sport fisherman.

The beautiful mountains around Cordova offer summer hiking and camping. Forest service cabins are available year-round for those who relish experiencing the wilderness. During the winter, Cordova offers the best of downhill and cross-country skiing. From the chair lift of Eyak Mountain high above Cordova you can literally ski across the mountaintops to eventually wind your way back down to the town.

Glennallen

Glennallen's strategic location at the junction of the Glenn and Richardson highways makes it the ideal stopping place for travelers visiting Valdez, exploring the historic mining towns of Chitina and Nabesna, or heading into the Wrangell Mountains towards McCarthy. Glennallen is 189 miles northeast of Anchorage and is a city growing in traveler services. These services include major auto repair, auto parts, service stations, and the broadcasting of road conditions on radio station KCAM. The Alaska state troopers, the Bureau of Land Management, and the Alaska Department of Fish and Game have offices in Glennallen. The city is also a fly-in base for guides and outfitters.

The many lakes in the area provide excellent fishing and boating. Boats and motors can be rented, and camping and hiking around the lakes are popular activities. Blueberries the size of grapes can be picked in the area. A drive to the face of Worthington Glacier south of Glennallen is well worth the time. This is one of the few glaciers in Alaska that lies next to the highway and can be viewed from extremely close range. Trout and salmon fishing are excellent in the Copper and Chitina rivers.

There are two lodges and a motel in Glennallen, and until the availability catches up with the demand, reservations are suggested for accommodations during the summer months. The friendly and courteous people of Glennallen and the beautiful mountain views make the city a delightful, as well as convenient, place to stay.

Homer

Homer is located on the southwestern Kenai Peninsula, 225 highway miles south of Anchorage. Situated on beautiful Kachemak Bay, Homer is a scenic settlement that is a haven for artists. The entire Homer area is fast becoming the year-round playground for Alaskans and tourists alike. Homer's easy highway accessibility and its modern airport and seaplane base make it an ideal resort location for those who wish to enjoy its scenery, mild climate, and numerous recreational possibilities.

From this charming, rustic city you can look across the bay to a shoreline indented with many fjords and coves reaching far into the rugged, glacier-capped peaks of the Kenai Mountains. To the west beyond Cook Inlet are the mountains and smoking volcanoes of the Aleutian Range. Atop a bluff behind the city are rolling lightly wooded hills and farmland with the snowcovered Kenai Mountains as a backdrop.

The Homer Spit, a sandbar jutting out five miles into the bay, is the center of the area's ocean fishing industry. There are hotels and restaurants located on the spit, and it is lined with many campgrounds and guide and charter services for fishing, sightseeing, hiking, and glacier walking. Halibut and salmon fishing excursions are very popular, and tours which include clamdigging, shrimping, and crabbing are also available. The restaurants and seafood shops serve nearly every variety of seafood in Alaska, including king crab.

Wildlife in the Homer area includes moose, Dall sheep, bear, ptarmigan, and grouse. Big game hunting is a specialty in the Homer area, and planes and guides can be hired in the city. Horseback trail rides along the beach and in the forests of the area are available, with overnight accommodations in guide camps.

The Kenai Fjords National Park and the Harding Ice Field are close by, while across Cook Inlet are Katmai National Monument and Lake Clark National Park and Preserve. Charters are available in Homer for excursions to all of these locations.

In addition to its role as a resort city, Homer has the possibility of becoming a city with a future in the oil industry as exploratory drilling continues in lower Cook Inlet. There is also an estimated 400 million tons of coal in the immediate vicinity of Homer. In fact, the erosion of the bluffs behind the city drops huge chunks of coal on the beaches, creating a plentiful supply of winter fuel for residents.

When planning a trip to Homer it is a good idea to make all reservations well in advance, especially during the busy summer months.

Kenai

The city of Kenai is situated on the upper western coast of the Kenai Peninsula on Cook Inlet. It is 158 miles south of Anchorage. The largest city on the Kenai Peninsula, Kenai was established in 1791 as a Russian fur trading post. Old Kenai and its Russian influences can still be seen in the city. The Russian Parish House still stands, and the nearby Russian Orthodox Church is still being used.

In 1957, oil was discovered in the area, and Kenai came to be known as the oil capital of Alaska. This is evidenced by the large oil and gas fields offshore and numerous large oil refineries and associated plants north of town. Fishing is the next largest industry, and tourism is becoming increasingly important.

The city of Kenai is busy and modern with all modern conveniences. The terrain surrounding Kenai is level and heavily forested with birch, aspen, and cottonwood. The view across Cook Inlet provides an unobstructed view of the mountains, most notably Mt. Illiamna, Mt. Spur, and Mt. Redoubt, the latter still an active volcano. There are numerous streams which empty into Cook Inlet. The Kenai River, one of the peninsula's best salmon fishing rivers, is noted for the large number of white beluga whales that can be seen swimming in and out of the river's mouth searching for fish. Moose and other wildlife are common sights along the highway.

Kenai can be reached by road via the eleven-mile Kenai Spur Road from the Sterling Highway.

Palmer

The city of Palmer is located in Alaska's famed Matanuska Valley, forty-two miles north of Anchorage. The fertile valley, nestled between the Talkeetna Mountains to the north and the Chugach Mountains to the south, is Alaska's prime agricultural region and is legendary for its oversize vegetables. As a result of the long hours of daylight in the summer, cabbages sometimes grow to a whopping seventy pounds. The picturesque farms with their two-story barns and snug farmhouses also produce most of Alaska's grain and cool-weather vegetable crops. There are a number of dairy farms tucked into this mountain cradle as well. The city of Palmer serves as the service center for over 9000 people, and the University of

Alaska maintains experimental farms and an agricultural research center and extension service in Palmer. Tours of the farms are conducted for visitors.

Many artists and craftsmen live in Palmer, and the area's unique qualities are reflected in their art. There are over fifty resorts in the mountains and on lakes and streams near the city that offer boating, golfing, fishing, hunting, and horseback riding. Trips to the historic Independence Gold Mine in the Hatcher Pass Recreation Area and tours of the Matanuska Glacier are popular side trips in the summer.

The Alaska State Fair in Palmer, an annual event attended by nearly 200,000 people, is held for eleven days each summer, ending on Labor Day. There are hundreds of agricultural and mechanical exhibits at the fair as well as a rodeo, a three-day state championship horse show, and a cabbage-weighing contest.

Seldovia

Seldovia is a small Alaskan fishing community located on the southwestern Kenai Peninsula near Kachemak Bay. There are no roads to Seldovia, but the town is a scheduled stop on the Marine Highway System, and the Homer Air Service provides flights from Homer, sixteen miles across the bay.

Seldovia, which has retained much of its old-world charm and tradition because of its inaccessibility to the rest of the peninsula by highway, is called the "City of Secluded Charm." Much of old Seldovia was built along a boardwalk on the slough, but since land subsided several feet during the 1964 earthquake, new homes and businesses have been built on higher ground.

In 1922 there was an abundance of herring in the area and several herring canneries were built. In fact, the name Seldovia is the Russian word for herring. However, the herring boom was short-lived. The harvesting of king crab is now the prominent industry, with crab processed almost year-round. A salmon cannery and more than fifty fox farms are also in the area.

Spaces for camping are available at Outside Beach about two miles from Seldovia, and although there are no tables, firepits, or water, there is a good freshwater stream nearby. Privately owned cabins are available for rent on a clam beach on Seldovia Bay; a hiking trail, good fishing, and beachcombing opportunities are nearby. There is also a hotel in Seldovia for those who do not like to rough it.

The Seward small boat harbor on Resurrection Bay is ringed by the beautiful Kenai Mountains. The harbor bustles with activity during the summer and is a good place to obtain fishing or sightseeing charters, or just to spend an afternoon. The Kenai Fjords National Park visitor center is located here as well and has information on sights to see and organized activities within the park.

Seward

Located on beautiful Resurrection Bay, Seward is on the east coast of the Kenai Peninsula, 127 miles south of Anchorage. Accessible by highway, it is a stop on the Marine Highway and is the southern terminus of the Alaska Railroad. The main industries are lumbering, fisheries, and government.

Seward is a friendly community nestled between two high mountain chains, the Kenai Mountains to the west and the Chugach Mountains to the north. It is situated along the boundary of the Chugach National Forest amid thick groves of cottonwood and spruce.

Recreational opportunities in and around Seward are excellent. Cruises in Resurrection Bay afford glimpses of whales, porpoises, sea otters, and sea lions. Trips to nearby Kenai Fjords National Park and the Harding Ice Field are available, as are charters to Pye and Chiswell Islands, the nesting grounds for hundreds of seabirds. These include tufted and horned puffins, rhinoceros and parakeet auklets, kittiwakes, and murres.

Fishing in the Resurrection River, Grayling Lake, and Grouse Lake will net the fisherman dolly varden, arctic char, grayling, and silver salmon. Flounder, halibut, and cod can be taken in Resurrection Bay.

Hiking trails include Two Lakes Trail, a mile-long loop along the base of Mt. Marathon, which affords beautiful views of the marina and north Resurrection Bay. The small boat harbor and ship-docking facilities, completely destroyed by tidal waves and fires during the Good Friday earthquake, are fully operational once again and provide a busy and colorful place to spend an afternoon. Shipping is again becoming increasingly important to the economy. There are several convenient campgrounds in the area around Seward and, of course, numerous campgrounds and miles of hiking trails in the Chugach National Forest nearby.

Seward is the home of the Alaska Skill Center, a vocational training center for the underprivileged, unemployed, and handicapped. It is also the location of the Institute of Marine Science maintained by the University of Alaska. Tours of these centers are available year-round.

Soldotna

Soldotna is located on the banks of the Kenai River at the junction of the Sterling Highway and the Kenai Spur Road, 150 miles south of Anchorage. The city is nestled snugly into the thick forests of the area, which makes it appear smaller than it really is because of the many homes and businesses tucked in behind the trees.

Soldotna is known as a top location for king salmon fishing. Trophy-size fish are often taken from the Kenai River. On weekends and holidays, many Anchorage residents head for the Soldotna area to fish, camp, and canoe on the lakes and rivers just north of the city. Soldotna's close proximity to the Kenai National Wildlife Refuge, good razor clam beaches, and several established river canoeing routes make it an ideal choice for some of the best recreational activities the Kenai Peninsula has to offer.

All modern conveniences and facilities are available in Soldotna, and its easy accessibility to major highways is unique in a state where there aren't that many roads. Campgrounds line the highways, and fishing and hunting guides are easily found for trips that don't necessarily require expensive air charters to remote locations, although these are also available.

Beachcombing is a popular activity on nearby Montague Island, which is on one of the main ocean currents that goes around the world, making the likelihood of finding very unusual objects a distinct possibility.

Special events in Soldotna include the Peninsula Winter Games in January, and the Clark Memorial Sled Dog Race and Alaska State Championship Sled Dog Race in February. Progress Days, held in July, is a two-day event featuring a rodeo, dance, talent show, motorcycle race, and an air show.

Talkeetna

The city of Talkeetna is located in the Susitna Valley 113 miles north of Anchorage at the junction of the Talkeetna, Chulitna, and Susitna rivers. The level-to-rolling land of the area is covered with stands of large birch, aspen, and cottonwood, and the view of Mt. McKinley and the Alaska Range to the northwest is magnificent. The name Talkeetna comes from an Indian word meaning "where the rivers meet." It is reached by automobile via a fourteen-mile spur road off the George Parks Highway. It is also a stop on the Alaska Railroad, which for many years was Talkeetna's only reliable means of ground transportation. The community was established as a mining and trapping settlement at the turn of the century, and miners built roads and worked the coal and silver mines in the Talkeetna Mountains to the east.

Talkeetna today is a jumping-off point for mountain climbing expeditions to Mt. McKinley, and climbers from all over the world congregate in the city during the summer. Talkeetna was home to Alaska's most famous bush pilot, the late Don Sheldon, who pioneered in flying climbers to and from glaciers on the mountain and who conducted search and rescue operations, sometimes under nearly impossible conditions.

The Fairview Inn is a favorite gathering place for the international crowd of mountain climbers that throngs to the tiny town of Talkeetna during the summer for climbing expeditions on Mt. McKinley. "Beautiful Downtown Talkeetna" hums with activity all summer long, and the B & K Trading Post across the street from the inn is another favorite hangout for residents and tourists alike.

The city is also the home of one of Alaska's well-known authors and journalists, Mary Carey, who has written of the excitement and danger inherent in flying the mountain in the early days of Alaska's statehood, and of the rigors of homesteading alone in the wilderness.

Four miles from Talkeetna is the Alascom Earth Station, a big dish nearly 100 feet tall, which monitors an orbiting communications satellite whose signals make live television possible in Alaska. Talkeetna is near the site of a proposed hydroelectric project on the Susitna River. The project is to be built in three stages as a source of electric power for the entire region.

The area offers good fishing and guided riverboat and raft trips. Flightseeing trips to surrounding areas and rockhounding in the Talkeetna Mountains are rewarding side trips in the summer.

Annual festivities in Talkeetna include Miner's Day in May and the Moose Dropping Festival in July, when contestants compete at throwing moose droppings. There is also an annual bluegrass music festival held each August and an annual cross-country ski race in the winter.

Valdez

Valdez is located on the north shore of Port Valdez in the Lowe River Valley of southcentral Alaska. The port is ice-free and open to navigation year-round. Valdez is the southern terminus of the Alyeska Pipeline and is 304 highway miles east of Anchorage.

Because of its pristine alpine beauty, Valdez is often referred to as the Switzerland of Alaska. It is a city surrounded by towering mountains and the crystal blue waters of Prince William Sound. Sportfishing is superb in the rushing clear waters of the many rivers, lakes, and streams nearby, and campers enjoy the convenience of the many campgrounds in and around Valdez, as well as forest service cabins on Prince William Sound.

Short trips and overnight tours to the Columbia Glacier are available from Valdez. This impressive glacier covers 440 square miles and is thirty stories high. Constantly calving, it sends towering chunks of ice into the waters of Prince William Sound. Tours of the Alyeska Pipeline Terminal across the bay from the city of Valdez are also conducted on a regular basis.

Within an easy drive of Valdez is the brutal beauty of Keystone Canyon. The canyon is dotted with high waterfalls, and an abandoned railroad tunnel stands here as mute evidence of the proposed railroad to the Kennicott Copper Mines. The site of violence between rival factions in 1907, the tunnel was never finished and the railroad never completed.

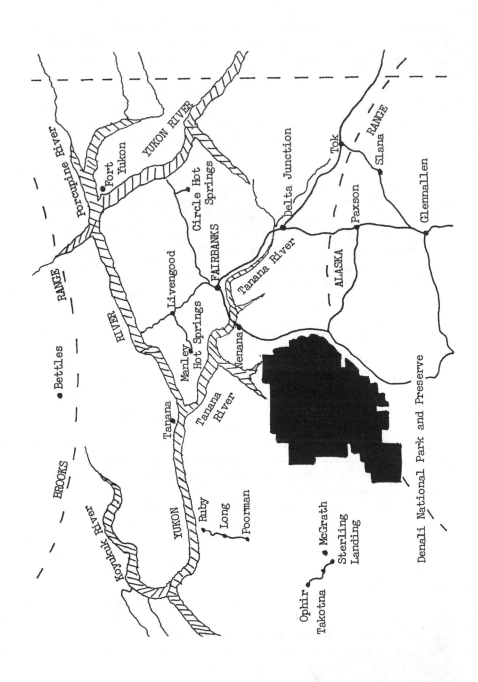

Nearby is Worthington Glacier, where glacier walks and high meadow picnics are popular.

There is highway access from Fairbanks to Valdez via the Richardson Highway, and access from Anchorage via the Glenn Highway to the Richardson Highway. Valdez is serviced by the Alaska Marine Highway from Seward and Cordova and has direct connections to Anchorage and the Kenai Peninsula via the railroad-ferry shuttle service from Portage and Whittier.

Interior Alaska

Delta Junction

Delta Junction is in the Tanana River Valley at milepost 1422 of the Alaska Highway at its junction with the Richardson Highway. It is 340 miles northeast of Anchorage. The Alaska Highway officially ends in Delta Junction, and the Richardson Highway continues on to Fairbanks, with the mileposts showing the distance from Valdez. The portion of road between Delta Junction and Fairbanks is often called the Alaska Highway, however, or the Alaska-Richardson Highway to avoid confusion.

Delta Junction is situated at the confluence of the Tanana and Delta rivers in a portion of the valley that is broad and forested. Forty to fifty miles to the southwest is the Alaska Range, and six major peaks are visible from Delta Junction. The city is located within the cold triangle of North America and does occasionally experience extremely cold temperatures. The record low is seventy-two degrees below zero, set in January of 1975. The weather is often windy—which to a Delta Junction resident means winds of twenty m.p.h. or more, gusting to eighty m.p.h. A wind of fifteen m.p.h. or less is considered a light breeze by locals. Since 1947 a single month has not gone by without at least one day with winds in excess of sixty m.p.h.

The Delta Junction area is one of the prime agricultural regions in the state of Alaska. In 1978 a state agricultural and development project opened over 60,000 acres of land to farming, and an additional 100,000 acres was opened in 1982. Major crops produced by delta farmers include barley, oats, grass seed, and wheat. Besides grain production, plans are being made for a major expansion of the livestock industry and for the building of a major grain ethanol production facility.

Opposite: The cities of interior Alaska.

The trans–Alaska pipeline came through Delta Junction in 1977. For many traveling the Alaska Highway, Delta Junction is the first opportunity to see and photograph the pipeline. The proposed natural gas pipeline is also scheduled to pass through the city.

The rivers and lakes in the delta area afford many recreational opportunities. Float trips may be taken by raft or canoe, and there is excellent sportfishing. There are several good campgrounds both in town and along the highway. There are several hundred buffalo in a preserve near Delta Junction that were transplanted to the area in the 1920s. Hunting of the bison is allowed each year by lottery permit. Keeping the buffalo in the preserve is a major problem. They have a great affinity for the grain grown by delta farmers, and they often become a nuisance by foraging in fields outside the boundaries of their preserve.

Fairbanks

Fairbanks is located in the heart of Alaska's Interior, 2361 miles from Seattle, Washington, at the northern end of the Alaska-Richardson Highway. It is 358 miles northeast of Anchorage via the George Parks Highway and is also the northern terminus of the Alaska Railroad.

Fairbanks lies in the Tanana Valley, on the banks of the Chena River, with the Tanana River to the south. Further south is the Alaska Range, visible on a clear day, and to the north, east, and west are low gold-bearing hills covered with birch and white spruce.

Fairbanks is known as the "golden heart city," and perhaps no other city in Alaska retains as much of the flavor of its frontier past as does the city of Fairbanks. The many old buildings and log structures contrast sharply with sleek modern department stores and office buildings, and the people are a mixture of newcomers, pioneers, miners, trappers, merchants, white collar and blue collar workers, and native Alaskans.

Fairbanks was founded by E.T. Barnette in 1901. At his request the city was named for a friend, Charles Warren Fairbanks, a senator from Indiana who later became vice president of the United States under Theodore Roosevelt. Barnette was traveling upriver by steamboat to establish a trading post in Tananacross, a settlement where the trail from Valdez to Eagle crossed the upper Tanana River. The steamboat was unable to continue up the Tanana because of rapids, and the low water level made travel up the Chena River impossible, so Barnette was stranded at the present site of Fairbanks, where he cached his goods. A year later, gold was discovered by Felix Pedro in the hills sixteen miles north of Barnette's cache. Barnette, an opportunist, decided to stay and establish a city. It was a wise decision. By 1906 the production of gold in the Fairbanks area was valued at nine million dollars and the population had grown to 3,541.

Milestones in the history of Fairbanks from that time were the establishing of the University of Alaska in 1915, the completion of the Alaska Railroad in 1923, and the completion of the Alaska Highway project in 1942. Military bases were set up during the Second World War and increased during the Korean conflict in the 1950s.

Today Fairbanks is the transportation hub for the north slope oil fields and arctic villages. The Fairbanks mining district is once again very active with the reopening of old claims, most notably along the Steese Highway north of town and in Ester five miles to the southwest. Government offices, the University of Alaska, military installations, and tourism are also important to the economy.

Fine hotels and restaurants, modern housing, and convenient shopping malls make Fairbanks a city where all the conveniences of modern living may be found. Its rich cultural life includes historians, painters, musicians, and actors. Poets and writers find a wealth of inspiration in their surroundings.

In Fairbanks you may take a riverboat cruise in one of Alaska's two big sternwheelers. The riverboats go past colorful mining towns, traplines, and Athabascan Indian fish wheels, and give the traveler a chance to learn about the Indian culture first hand. Tours can be taken to the kennels where many Alaskan sled dogs are kept throughout the year and demonstrations of their skills can be witnessed. A vaudeville show depicting "the Shooting of Dan McGrew," the famous work of Robert Service, can be seen in the small mining town of Ester on the banks of Cripple Creek. The Malemute Saloon where the show is held still has sawdust floors and sourdough bartenders.

The University of Alaska, the northernmost institution of higher learning in the world, has numerous exhibits of native arts and crafts, gold nuggets, and many kinds of fossils in their museum. A visit to the Alyeska Pipeline, which carries Alaskan crude to Valdez, is a major attraction, as is Alaskaland, a pioneer park with historical reconstructions of gold rush camps, native villages, and mining towns as they were during the gold rush era. North Pole, Alaska, and the official Santa Claus House are close by and well worth a visit.

From Fairbanks, planes can be chartered to fly to any number of remote-access villages or national parks such as Gates of the Arctic or Yukon Flats. It is a short drive to the several hot springs resorts in the area, or to Eagle, where float trips into the Yukon-Charley Rivers National Park originate.

Fort Yukon

Situated at the confluence of the Yukon and Porcupine rivers, Fort Yukon, with a population of 600, is the largest Athabascan Indian village in Alaska. Established as a fur trading post in 1847, it is also the oldest community in Alaska's Interior. It is known today for its furs, fish wheels, salmon drying racks, and Athabascan beadwork. The town is ten miles north of the Arctic Circle and has one inn, a restaurant, and several grocery stores.

Hot Springs Resorts

Circle Hot Springs and Chena Hot Springs are two of Alaska's prime resort cities. Located east of Fairbanks, both resorts are easily reached by highway and both offer campgrounds and picnic areas, hot mineral baths, swimming, hotel rooms, and pioneer cabins. There is a lodge at each resort with dining facilities and organized indoor activities. The surrounding countryside offers opportunities for gold panning, camping, boating, hiking, and berry picking.

Manley Hot Springs is west of Fairbanks at the end of the Elliot Highway. There is a public campground near the hot springs and a roadhouse where overnight accommodations are available. A four-story resort hotel built here by Frank Manley in 1907 did much business with miners in the Eureka and Tofty mining districts during the gold mining era.

Nenana

Nenana, a city of about 500 people, is located at the confluence of the Nenana and Tanana rivers, fifty miles southwest of Fairbanks. The name Nenana is an Indian word meaning "a good place to camp between the rivers." In early days, Nenana was a trading post and supply point for river travelers and fur traders. Today it is the home port of the tug and barge fleet that in summer carries tons of freight, fuel, and supplies to villages along the Tanana and Yukon rivers. During the construction of the Alaska Railroad, Nenana was set up as the northern construction base for railroad workers. President Warren G. Harding drove a golden railroad spike here when the railroad was completed. Nenana is still an important rail barge facility for the Interior.

Nenana is famous all over Alaska as the center of the state's biggest guessing game, the Nenana Ice Classic. Legal only for Alaskan residents, this contest offers an average annual cash payoff of over $100,000 to the person who can guess the exact moment of ice breakup in the Tanana River. Surging ice dislodges a tripod and an attached line stops a time clock at the moment of breakup. In midwinter, the setting up of the tripod is the focal point for Tripod Days, an extravaganza of winter races, exhibits, and contests.

Tok

Tok is a city of 800 at the junction of the Alaska and Glenn highways. A visitor center in Tok, operated by the state Department of Public Safety, maintains an extensive inventory of brochures and information covering nearly every part of the state. The center offers free coffee to travelers and is open from seven a.m. until ten p.m. every day during the summer.

Tok was established as a construction camp for the Alaska Highway in 1942. The city was then called Tokyo Camp because it was near the Tokyo river. Patriotism during the war shortened the name to Tok, and today the city remains the major overland point of entry into Alaska. Tok is important as a trade and service center for people traveling the Alaska Highway. There is an auto repair and wrecker service here as well as several gas stations, motels, and restaurants. There are gift shops and sporting goods stores, and three campgrounds with laundry facilities. The campgrounds offer slide presentations and movies. Activities in Tok revolve around things typically Alaskan, like gold panning and dog sled demonstrations. There are also square dances and softball games, and festivals on Memorial Day and Labor Day that include car and boat races. The Fourth of July usually sees a big parade with floats, contests, and picnicking.

Southwestern Alaska

Kodiak

Kodiak Island, roughly the size of Connecticut, is in the Gulf of Alaska, some 250 miles south of Anchorage. It is east of the Alaska Peninsula and separated from it by Shelikof Strait, which is thirty to fifty miles wide. The city of Kodiak is located near the northeastern tip of the island and is the nation's third largest commercial fishing center. It is the birthplace of the king crab fishing industry. Kodiak was the first Russian settlement in America and is Alaska's most historic island. The city offers modern, well-appointed accommodations in a rugged frontier setting. Most buildings

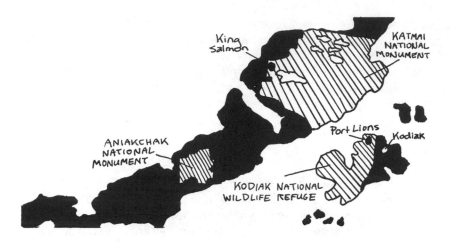

The cities of the southwest.

are new, as much of Kodiak was rebuilt after the 1964 earthquake when huge tidal waves washed over the city.

Kodiak's mild, wet climate has contributed to its lush vegetation, giving the island the reputation of being Alaska's "Emerald Isle." Precipitation averages about sixty inches a year, and the long, cool summers are often rainy. Winter temperatures seldom drop to zero, and in the city itself, snow is the exception rather than the rule. This is not true, however, of the mountains. Kodiak Island is mountainous, with a north-south divide rising to heights of 2000 to 4000 feet. It has over 800 miles of jagged coastline with many bays, inlets, and smaller islands. To the southeast of Kodiak occupying the lush land between the ocean and the mountains are several large cattle ranches. One of these, the Kodiak Cattle Company, has a large herd of Black Angus–Herefords and Belted Galloways on 21,000 acres of land. Also raised here are horses, buffalo, and beefalo, a cross between buffalo and beef cattle that yields meat with a very high protein content.

The southwestern two-thirds of the island is set aside as the Kodiak National Wildlife Refuge and is the home of the world-famous Kodiak brown bear, the largest living carnivorous animal on earth. There are approximately 2000 of these huge bears on the island, and hunters come from all over the world to get trophy-size animals. Local big-game hunting guides provide guiding services and accommodations in their camps. Other species in the refuge include Dall sheep, moose, reindeer, mountain goat, deer and elk. Sport and game fishing is also superb in the many rivers, lakes, and streams on Kodiak Island.

Port Lions

Located just west of Kodiak, Port Lions is a town of about 300 people and is a regular stop on the Alaska Marine Highway. Originally called Afognak, the city was destroyed by tidal waves in 1964 and was rebuilt twenty-five miles away with the help of the district Lions Club – hence the city's name. There are several churches, a motel, and an airstrip in Port Lions. Air service to the town is available from Kodiak.

King Salmon

This small town of 545 people is located on the Alaska Peninsula near Katmai National Monument. There is scheduled airline service to King Salmon from other Alaskan cities. Access into the park from King Salmon is by local road and by floatplane.

Naknek Lake, Illiamna Lake, Becharof Lake, and Ugashik Lake are several large lakes In the area known for their superb sportfishing. King Salmon is the usual point of entry to these lakes, as well as to the lodges and guide camps that exist around the lakes and in the park. In addition to sportfishing, recreational activities in the area include wildlife viewing, canoeing, kayaking, backpacking, and photography.

The city of King Salmon has a post office, a hotel, and two restaurants. There is also an air force installation here, an office of the Alaska state troopers, and the headquarters of Katmai National Monument.

Western Alaska

Bethel

Bethel, a city of 3,683 people, is western Alaska's largest community and is located on the banks of the Kuskokwim River, where it flows into Kuskokwim Bay. Bethel is the heart city of the Yukon-Kuskokwim Delta. The Yukon and Kuskokwim rivers meander across this broad fertile plain, where countless lakes, ponds, streams, and sloughs constitute one of the most significant waterfowl breeding areas in North America.

The commercial and administrative headquarters for the bay area are located in Bethel, where barges and airliners bring in goods during the summer that are then taken by small boat or bush plane to the many villages scattered throughout the region. The commercial fishing industry (primarily salmon and herring) contributes heavily to the economy. Most of the residents of Bethel are engaged in fishing or transportation, or are

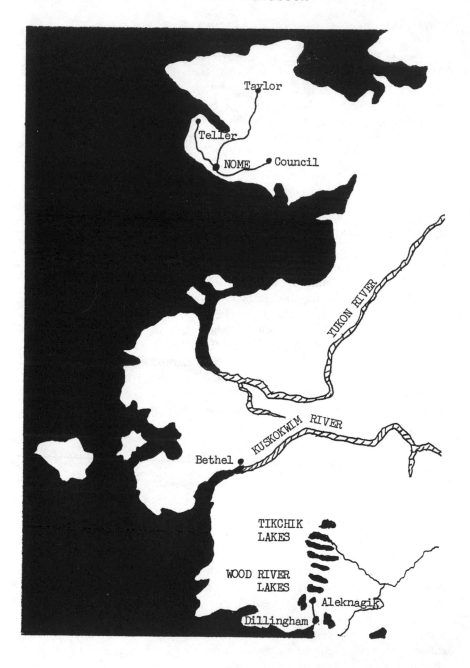

The cities of the west.

employed by one of the growing number of private industries, native corporations, and government offices.

Accommodations in Bethel include one hotel, several restaurants,
and an air charter service for flights to the Yukon Delta National Wildlife
Refuge. There is commercial air service to Bethel daily from Anchorage
and several times per week from Nome.

Council

The community of Council is located at the end of a graveled road,
about seventy miles east of Nome. The town sits on the left bank of the
Niukluk River, and the twenty or so inhabitants depend on subsistence
hunting and fishing for their living. Council was established in the late
1800s and was once the center of the Council mining district. A reac-
tivated gold dredge operates in the area, and the sportfishing is superb.
A local fishing camp offers guided fishing and photography expeditions,
with accommodations at the camp.

Dillingham

Located on Bristol Bay in western Alaska at the confluence of the
Nushagak and Wood rivers, Dillingham is the center of industry for the
entire Bristol Bay area. Cargo ships bring supplies into the Dillingham harbor for distribution to the many villages scattered throughout the region.
With a population of about 2000 people, Dillingham, it has been said, has
more millionaires per capita than anywhere else in the United States.

Streams and rivers flowing into the bay are the site of the largest red
salmon spawning grounds in the world, and the Nushagak River produces
the area's major pink salmon run. Dillingham is the major center for fish
processing in the Bristol Bay area. Populations of sheefish and whitefish
are also of importance to the processing industry.

Trapping and tourism are very important aspects of the city's
economy. The close proximity of Dillingham to the Wood River–Tikchik
Lakes State Park makes it an ideal place from which to arrange trips into
the park. The opportunities for fishing and boating on two separate
systems of interconnected lakes are limitless, and the area is one of the
most beautiful in the state, with mountains to the west and tundra to the
east. The beautiful parallel lakes were formed by glaciers that are no
longer present in the region. Numerous wilderness lodges operate within
the park and throughout the entire surrounding area. Most of these lodges

offer all accommodations and equipment for sportfishing vacations; some offer hunting and river trips as well.

Nome

The city of Nome is located on the south coast of the Seward Peninsula, facing Norton Sound in the Bering Sea. The city is protected by a seawall nearly 3400 feet long, made of giant granite boulders trucked in at a cost of almost one million dollars.

Nome is a city proud of its rich history. It was established during the gold rush days in 1899, when it became a tent city with nearly 20,000 prospectors seeking their fortunes in Nome's gold-bearing creeks and on its black sand beaches. Destroyed by fire in 1905 and again in 1934, Nome has survived to become a growing hub of commerce for the Seward Peninsula. The mining of gold is still an important contribution to the economy, as is tourism.

Thousands of people come to Nome each year to experience the flavor of "Gold Rush Nome" and to enjoy the native culture in the city and in nearby native villages. March is a month of great excitement, as it marks the beginning of the Iditarod Trail Dog Sled Race, the world's longest and toughest race over the frozen tundra, rivers, mountains, and ice-locked seacoast between Anchorage and Nome. This historic trail originally came all the way from Seward and was blazed by Alaskan natives to move mail and supplies from the ice-free port at Seward to the gold fields of Nome. Millions of dollars' worth of gold from Nome was transported to the port by dog teams returning along the same route. In 1925 a portion of the trail was used by twenty mushers to relay diptheria serum to Nome.

March also brings the excitement of the grueling 200-mile Nome–Golovin–Nome snowmachine race. Special summer events in Nome include the annual Memorial Day Bering Sea Swim, the Midnight Sun Festival in June, and the annual Fourth of July parade.

Taylor

A graveled road leads north from Nome some eighty-six miles to the Kougarok Mine, and beyond another thirty-five miles to the community of Taylor, which was once the center of the Kougarok Gold Mining District. The area around the mine offers excellent fishing and moose-hunting possibilities.

Teller

At the end of a gravel road seventy-two miles northwest of Nome is the city of Teller, with a population of about 200 people. Teller is known for its placer gold mining and its reindeer herding. Teller has a trading post, an air taxi service, telephone service, and a school. The trading post carries large stocks of ivory for ivory carving, and many native crafts. Wildlife in the area includes whales, seals, and polar bears. The road offers good views of the reindeer herds, which are owned by the native corporation and are sold to provide meat for the Seward Peninsula.

Arctic Alaska

Barrow

Located on the coast of the Chukchi Sea, 550 miles north of Fairbanks, Barrow is the second largest native settlement in North America. Barrow is truly the land of the midnight sun. The sun rises in Barrow on May 10 and does not set again until August 2. In winter the sun disappears at noon on November 18 and is not seen again until noon on January 24.

Barrow is the seat of government for the North Slope Borough, the world's largest municipal government in terms of area. The borough covers 88,000 square miles but has a population of only 4,200. The city of Barrow is built on a barren stretch of beach that rims the Arctic Ocean. The houses are small wooden frame structures heated by natural gas from the gas fields nearby. The city has no paved streets or sidewalks because of the permanently frozen ground, and no underground water or sewer systems for the same reason. During the summer, water is transported from a small lake near the city, and in winter, ice is melted for water.

The native economy is based on whaling, sealing, fishing, and walrus hunting. The city has a small hospital, a construction firm, a native-owned hotel with a restaurant, three grocery stores, and a bakery. Barrow has recently added a new Mexican restaurant, where meals average $15 a plate.

There is regularly scheduled airline service to Barrow from both Anchorage and Fairbanks. Air transportation is the only way to get to Barrow, for there is no passenger service on oceangoing vessels that far north. Local air charter services can be hired for sightseeing in the area.

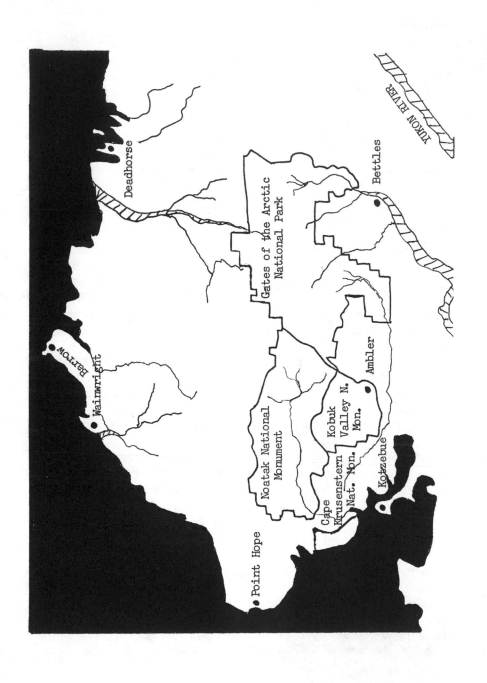

Bettles

Bettles is a small arctic village and airfield located on the Koyukuk River in arctic Alaska, just south of Gates of the Arctic National Park and Preserve. Bettles Field is considered a jumping-off point for trips into the park, and as such has scheduled air service from Fairbanks. Access into the park is then by air charter from Bettles.

Deadhorse

Deadhorse came into being when the North Slope Haul Road, now the Dalton Highway, was constructed to accommodate the oil operations at Prudhoe Bay. Located a few miles to the south of Prudhoe Bay, Deadhorse has a general store and several camps with accommodations for visitors. Rooms are expensive and should be reserved well in advance. There is regularly scheduled air service to Deadhorse from Anchorage and Fairbanks, and several package tours are available to the North Slope area. It is normally not possible to drive the Dalton Highway as far as Deadhorse. Only persons with a special permit are allowed to drive past Disaster Creek near Dietrich. Permits are issued by the Director of Maintenance and Operations, Department of Transportation, 2301 Peger Road, Fairbanks AK 99701.

Kotzebue

Kotzebue is located on the northwest shore of the Baldwin Peninsula in Kotzebue Sound. The city is near the Kobuk and Noatak rivers and is about 180 miles from the Siberian mainland. Eighty percent of Kotzebue's population of 2,470 are natives who rely on subsistence fishing and hunting for their living. Hunting is still done using traditional dogsleds for transportation, but more often snowmachines are used. Government construction and tourism also add much to the economy.

The houses in Kotzebue are much like those in Barrow – small wooden frame structures with no sidewalks in front. There are no paved streets in Kotzebue except for a two-mile state highway that runs through the middle of town. Front Street consists of a gravel beach that runs the length of the waterfront next to the many drying racks for fish and game that are processed right on the beach. Parts of the city have a water and sewer system.

Opposite: *The cities of the Arctic.*

One of the best places in Alaska to shop for jade is in Kotzebue at the Jade Shop. The jade comes from the Arctic near the Kobuk, Dall, and Shungnak rivers, and at Jade Mountain. It is found in Alaska in various shades of green, brown, black, yellow, white, and red. The most valuable jades found are black, white, and green jades that are marbled.

The city has a native-owned hotel with a restaurant, a small hospital, a television station, and a radio station that serves as a bush message center.

Some of the best hunting and fishing country in the state is found near Kotzebue, and bush flights can be chartered for this purpose. The Kobuk River area, the Arctic's most scenic, is nearby in rugged mountain country with several remote, unspoiled native villages scattered along the river-banks. Wildlife includes sheep, moose, caribou, and grizzly bear. There is also a reindeer herd, numbering about 6000 animals, owned by the native corporation to provide meat for the peninsula.

Point Hope

Point Hope, a village of 544 people, lies on the shores of the Chukchi Sea, about 273 miles north of Nome. It is a site believed to have been con-tinuously inhabited for longer than any other site in North America, as evidenced by ancient native artifacts that have been found there.

The natives who live in Point Hope today depend for their living on the whaling industry and on tourism. There are two lodges in the village for visitors, and guide services for wilderness excursions are available. There is airline service daily during the summer.

7. Flying to Alaska

A trip to Alaska is one of the most exciting adventures that can be undertaken by pilots and nonpilots alike, but the added thrill it provides a flyer makes it an experience never to be forgotten. Seeing this still unspoiled land from the air will take your breath away. The panorama stretches for endless miles, treating the eyes to the rugged beauty that is truly Alaskan. And the opportunity to touch down and be part of it all makes the sight that much more rewarding. The people of Alaska have the same sense of hospitality and genuineness that must have been prevalent during America's pioneer days. Wherever you may fly, you will find a warm welcome and people willing to share their rich heritage with you.

Increasing numbers of pilots from all over North America have been flying the Alaska Highway to Alaska. The highway serves as a helpful guidepath for VFR flight and can be used for emergency landings if necessary. There are also gravel airstrips all along the highway at regular intervals. With adequate preparation and preflight planning the flight can be the least hazardous and least complex of any international flight. Food, water, and medical facilities are available even in the smaller towns and there is no language problem. There are excellent motels and camping facilities all along the route and recreational opportunities at almost every landing site along the way. The key to a wonderful trip is proper planning, and perhaps even boning up on a few skills such as pilotage and slow flight maneuvers that are rarely needed anymore in the lower forty-eight. Sharpening up mountain flying skills is also extremely helpful.

Flying to and within Alaska is somewhat different from flying anywhere else in the United States. Extreme contrasts of terrain and weather may be encountered when flying in northwest Canada and Alaska, as well as a distinct lack of human habitation in all areas that do not lie directly along the highway. The land mass is a seemingly endless sprawl of mountains, some of which are permanently snowcapped. The overland terrain between the Canadian border and the Alaska border is dominated by two major mountain ranges, the Rocky Mountains and the

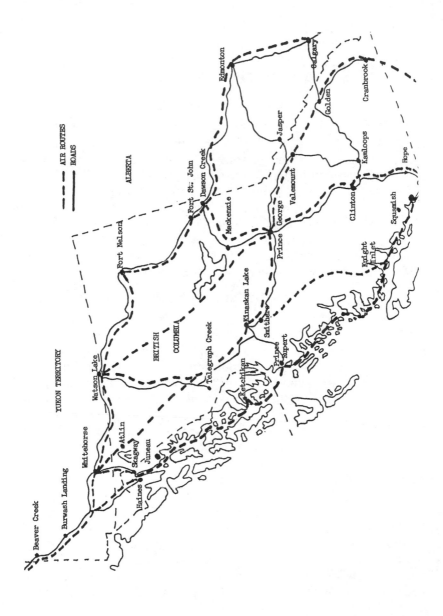

AIR ROUTES
ROADS

YUKON TERRITORY

ALBERTA

BRITISH
COLUMBIA

Beaver Creek
Burwash Landing
Whitehorse
Atlin
Skagway
Juneau
Haines
Watson Lake
Telegraph Creek
Kinaskan Lake
Smithers
Prince Rupert
Ketchikan
Port Nelson
Port St. John
Dawson Creek
Mackenzie
Prince George
Valemount
Clinton
Knight Inlet
Squamish
Edmonton
Jasper
Golden
Calgary
Cranbrook
Kamloops
Hope

Coastal Mountains, which extend in a northwesterly direction roughly parallel to one another. The highest mountains lie along the coast, ranging up to nearly 20,000 feet near the Alaskan border. These mountains form a solid barrier from Vancouver, B.C., all the way to Valdez, Alaska. The Rocky Mountain range is more extensive, with its highest mountain lying along the border of British Columbia and Alberta and reaching heights of about 12,000 feet. Inland from the coast and in the Rockies there are countless river valleys, with streams flowing in all directions. The complexity of the mountain ranges makes it difficult for small aircraft to depend on VFR radio navigation, and most general aviation aircraft do not have the capability to fly IFR safely over this section of the country, where minimum en route altitudes may be over 10,000 feet above sea level. The prevalence of cloud layers in the valleys during much of the year may oblige the VFR pilot to fly at relatively low altitudes, which limits his gliding and radio transmission range in the event of engine malfunction. The predominance of thick timber and uneven terrain underscores the problems of an emergency landing for the pilot who is unfamiliar with the area.

The network of VOR NAVAIDS in the United States is so extensive that many pilots have never attempted to fly from one point to another depending only upon ground reference and a chart. In Canada and Alaska it is possible to fly for a hundred miles without passing a town, and the problem of staying on course can become critical. The problem is worsened by the use of an unfamilar chart and by the presence of an environment with few useful landmarks. Many of the routes follow waterways or river valleys which appear to have an infinite number of forks and junctions. One wrong turn can lead the unwary pilot into a maze of twisting valleys amid steep mountain slopes, and culminate in a box canyon or the floor of an overcast. "Shortcuts" in an area such as this can be an open invitation to disaster, and even pilots following the road can mistake a logging road for the graveled highway without the proper charts.

To fly the overland route VFR to Alaska you should have at least a dozen Canadian aeronautical charts or half a dozen WAC charts. You should also have the appropriate U.S. sectionals for Alaska, and you should study the Alaska supplement to the *Airman's Information Manual* for required equipment and supplies. It is important to plan to make the trip in easy stages and to decide beforehand that you will refuse to hurry, or to fly at all in marginal weather.

Opposite: *Air routes to Alaska.*

This small plane was spotted filling up at the Chulitna River Lodge Gas Station on the George Parks Highway. It is not uncommon for planes to land on highways in Alaska in areas where there are no convenient runways. Most lodges have aviation fuel as well as fuel for more traditional highway vehicles.

Routes East of the Rocky Mountains

Alaska-bound pilots east of the Rockies usually make Calgary, Alberta, their point of entry into Canada and then follow the main highway via Edmonton to Dawson Creek. This is a 550-mile flight over fairly open, flat land.

Dawson Creek is the starting point of the 1,520-mile Alaska Highway that leads to Fairbanks. The highway was carved across the Rockies at an average elevation of about 2,500 feet above sea level. It forms the floor of a corridor with an average width of about six or seven miles, and with walls that have an average height of about 5,500 feet above sea level. Milepost number one is at Dawson Creek, but flight planning is better accomplished at Fort St. John, a short forty-seven-mile hop away. Fort St. John has an Aeradio station for flight assistance and trained meterologists for weather briefings. For the 300-mile trip on to Fort Nelson from Fort St. John, the VFR pilot can fly directly along the airway or along the highway. The terrain rises imperceptively en route, and at Midway the road elevation is considerably higher than at either Fort St. John or Fort Nelson.

After Fort Nelson the highway begins its westward penetration of the Rockies and is soon overshadowed by mountain peaks of over 7,500 feet. Both communications and navigational radio exist along the remainder of the route, but the VFR pilot who is flying within the corridor will have inconsistent contact at best with radio stations because of the terrain. Clouds tend to form along the peaks and frequently solidify into an overcast that may force the unwary VFR pilot into a collision with rising ground.

The 300-mile stretch between Fort Nelson and Watson Lake is notorious for very abrupt changes in weather, from blue skies to completely overcast, from calm air to severe turbulence and wind shear. Near Muncho Lake the highway makes a right-angle turn; several pilots have become lost after missing this turn and following an old mining road.

The next segment presents the pilot with an even narrower corridor as the Alcan Highway weaves its way between 6,000- and 7,000-foot peaks along the British Columbia–Yukon border, then moves sharply northwest in the direction of Whitehorse. Adverse atmospheric and mineral conditions, as well as terrain obstacles, frequently interrupt radio signals for low-flying aircraft. Nevertheless, most pilots of light planes find their greatest safety in flying low enough to keep the highway clearly in view, and to thereby avoid wandering off over old logging roads or apparent short cuts.

Leaving Whitehorse, pilots must take care not to be misled by the northerly route to Braeburn, but to follow the Alaska Highway as it moves northwest to Burwash and to Beaver Creek near the Alaskan border. Between the highway and the Pacific Coast, an enormous glacier field extends, hundreds of miles long, dominated by Mount Logan (elevation 19,850 feet). To the northwest, in the direction of Fairbanks, a broad river valley opens up, affording the pilot uninterrupted VOR radio navigation on into Alaska.

Routes West of the Rocky Mountains

Pilots flying to Alaska from points west of the Rocky Mountains have four basic routes to follow, depending upon whether they cross the border into Canada along the Pacific Coast, or inland. The shortest flight is directly up the Pacific Coast of British Columbia, about 700 miles from Seattle to Ketchikan. Most experienced pilots agree, however, that this route can be flown safely only in seaplanes or floatplanes that are piloted by persons with at least some knowledge of the area. The jagged coastline with its innumerable islets, inlets, and fjords is one of the easiest places in the world to get lost, particularly when the sea fog obscures visibility — as it does most of the time. The VFR flight path follows the shipping lanes, passing between Vancouver Island and the British Columbia mainland for about half of the journey north. After leaving Point Hardy, the route proceeds along narrow winding passageways to Prince Rupert, a distance of about 300 miles without a single land-plane airport. The more favorable beaches for landing are shown on WAC charts by a wavy line; however, the shore terrain is always susceptible to change from landslides, flooding, winds, and logjams. Personal experience and advice from veteran pilots is the best safety cushion for flying the Inside Passage. Some Alaskan pilots who regularly fly up and down the coast use aircraft with minimal instrument panels, sometimes even foregoing gyro instruments, because of their unwillingness to depend on anything but their own eyes and their knowledge of the terrain below. They fly close to the surface at all times and put the plane down whenever visibility becomes uncertain.

The second route out of Vancouver follows the Strait of Georgia as far as Knight Inlet, then veers north to Smithers, Kinaskan Lake, and on to Watson or Whitehorse. At 995 miles, it is the shortest of three overland routes to Whitehorse, but it is recommended only for pilots of float aircraft who have had experience flying over remote bush country. The first seventy miles takes you through a narrow pass in the Coastal Mountains ringed by high mountains over 10,000 feet, with a minimum recommended en route altitude of 5000 feet above sea level. After the pass the route follows more open country to Smithers. On the whole, the terrain is rugged, human habitation scarce, and there may be intermittent loss of radio communications and an absence of recognizable landmarks.

The normal choice for wheel-equipped coast pilots is to fly east from Vancouver along the Fraser River Valley for eighty-five miles to Hope, then head directly north by way of Clinton to Prince George, a distance of 445 miles. This route follows Transport Canada airways and main highways and rivers for the entire distance. VOR communications are good, and full-facility airports are located at Abbotsford, Williams Lake and Quesnel. There are private airstrips at Cache Creek, Clinton, Green Lake, 100-Mile House and 108-Mile House, and several emergency strips in between. From Vancouver to Hope, the suggested minimum altitude is 3000 feet; from Hope to Cache Creek it is 5000 feet. There can be rapidly changing weather conditions in the segment from Hope to Cache Creek, with quick wind shifts and turbulent downflowing air, especially on hot summer days. From Cache Creek to Prince George the route is over rolling country that forms the Central Interior Plateau.

For pilots beginning their flight in the vicinity of Spokane, the normal route makes the first Canadian stop at Cranbrook in the southeast corner of British Columbia, then runs toward Alaska along one of the river valleys that run parallel to the Rockies. The longest of these valleys, known as the Rocky Mountain Trench, runs from Cranbrook to Prince George, a distance of 450 miles. The highest ground elevation is 4,000 feet above sea level, and the minimum recommended en route altitude is 5,000 feet above sea level. Most of the route follows a highway, river, and railroad so that it is difficult to get lost. Good radio facilities are located at either end, and broadcast radio stations are located at two midway points, Golden and Valemont. There is one 100-mile stretch between Boat Encampment and Valemont where there is no highway or railroad below — only a narrow river winding its way through wild, mountainous terrain. Weather is changeable here, and severe turbulence and rapidly lowering ceilings are possible.

From Prince George, the preferred route is to follow the highway and railroad to Fort St. John and continue up the Alaska Highway. Although not very high, Pine Pass, midway between Prince George and St. John, is noted for strong winds, at times associated with severe turbulence. A combination of low-altitude turbulence and very strong winds aloft can make this pass virtually impassable for light aircraft on occasion. At such times it may be necessary to detour around the mountains by following the Peace River westward to Hudson Hope and then following the northernmost segment of the trench on up to Watson Lake and the Alaska Highway.

Continuing along the trench from Prince George to Watson Lake is a shortcut to Alaska that follows a clear valley all the way. However, except for the first 100 miles or so, there is no highway. Between Mackenzie and Watson Lake, a distance of about 390 miles, there are no radio aids, no fuel, and only small or emergency airstrips, which are not always easy to spot from the air. This route is recommended in good weather only, and only during daylight hours.

From Prince George it is also possible to head west, following a highway some 100 miles to Smithers, and then fly north to Watson Lake by way of Bell-Irving Pass and Kinaskan Lake. The pass is very narrow and about thirty miles long, at an elevation of 4,000 feet above sea level. The adjoining mountains are over 10,000 feet, and the pass area is notorious for bad weather. Beyond the pass there are no airstrips except for one about fifteen miles south of Kinaskan Lake, and no NAVAIDS. There are three airstrips along the 192 miles from Kinaskan Lake to Watson Lake on the Alaska Highway, but no radio aids or NAVAIDS exist en route. If the weather is clear, it is also possible to fly directly from Kinaskan Lake to Whitehorse via Atlin, some 275 miles over very high terrain, with one small airstrip at Telegraph Creek in the Cassiar. Recommended en route altitude is 7,000 feet above sea level. Again there are no radio or NAVAID installations along the route. There are numerous lakes suitable for seaplane use.

Most people make Northway their point of entry into Alaska, and schedule a restful stop for customs, fuel, food and flight planning. The route from Northway to Fairbanks follows the broad Tanana River Valley and the Alaska Highway, with adequate landing facilities and good communications along the entire route. For those pilots going to Anchorage, there are still a few mountain passes to get through. The most comfortable way is to fly the Alaska Highway to the Tok Junction, and then pick up the Glenn Highway south through Mentasta Pass to Glennallen. At Glennallen, the Glenn Highway bends to southwest on its way to Tehetna Pass and the Matanuska Valley. A maze of little airports in the Sheep Mountain area at the mouth of the Matanuska Glacier provides emergency landing areas if weather should close in. The highway runs the entire length of the valley through Chickaloon Pass to Palmer, where the road turns to the south and goes into Anchorage.

The pilot who chooses to fly his own plane to Alaska has a tremendous advantage once he has reached his destination. The Alaskan road network is very small and is limited to the southcentral region and portions of the interior region. Most areas of the state are inaccessible to motor vehicles, and even in areas where there are roads, there are many places to see that can be reached only by air. Remote lodges, even those accessible only by floatplane, are often near a land airport, which eliminates most of the considerable expense that would otherwise be required to get there. The amount of wildlife that can be seen (and often photographed) from a small plane is startling—much, much more than is seen from an automobile.

For those who would enjoy the company and added security of traveling with an organized group, there is a unique tour offered by a California-based tour group called Freebird Tours. They offer twenty-one-day flying tours to Alaska for pilots who wish to fly their own planes yet do not want to undertake such a long journey completely on their own. Scheduled accommodations and excursions are offered at group discounts along the way, but there are no locked-in schedules. You can plan your trip around the tour with a high degree of individuality, utilizing any or all group benefits as you wish. The freedom of choice is yours. Pilots from all over the United States have taken advantage of this method of flying to Alaska, and at the end of the tour, most people find they have made close friends and shared experiences with others who have the same interests as they. There is usually only enough time for three tours per summer, so reservations should be made as early in the season as possible. Complete information may be obtained by writing to this address:

Freebird Tours
975 Valley Blvd.
Los Angeles, CA 90032
Phone: (213) 225-0591
or: (818) 336-2427

A Piper Supercub on floats, flying above Lake Hood Floatplane Base in Anchorage. Many of the small bush air carriers are based here; they fly passengers to all parts of Alaska in the summertime for sightseeing and fishing trips.

Information Sources

A number of publications, in addition to maps and charts, are a must for anyone flying to Alaska. The following is a list of places to write, not only for necessary maps and charts, but for other helpful information as well.

Two publications that are indispensable in planning a flight through Canada to Alaska are "Air Tourist Information Canada" and "Flying the Alaska Highway through Canada." These booklets are available from:

Aeronautical Information Services
Place de Village
Ottawa, Ontario K1A ON8
Canada

A catalog of aeronautical charts and related publications can be obtained from:

U.S. Department of Commerce
NOAA National Ocean Survey
Distribution Center (C44)
Riverdale MD 20840

or from:

Canada Map Office
Department of Energy, Mines and Resources
615 Booth Street
Ottawa, Ontario K1A OE9
Canada

When ordering, the things you will need are

The Alaska Supplement
Canadian DND Flight Information Publication
VFR Supplement
Northern Supplement
World Aeronautical Charts
Appropriate WAC charts and/or Sectionals

There are two main sources of flight information in Alaska. Two publications, "Flight Tips for Alaskan Tourists" and "Cold Weather Operations of Aircraft," may be obtained from:

Federal Aviation Administration
Accident Prevention Specialist
701 C Street, Box 14
Anchorage AK 99513

The Alaska Division of Tourism has a package of information especially formulated for those flying their own plane to Alaska. When requesting this package, be sure to specify the type of aircraft you will be flying, the season of the year you intend to visit, the length of your intended stay, whether you will be camping out, and the areas of Alaska you intend to visit. Write to:

Alaska Division of Tourism
Pouch E
Juneau AK 99811

A book called *Your Alaskan Flight Plan* by Don and Julia Downie (TAB Books, Inc.) is very helpful. The authors have flown the various routes many times and have prepared this thorough handbook covering everything from preflight planning to detailed tips on every aspect of the flight, including landing fields photographed from the air. This book may be obtained by writing to:

TAB Books, Inc.
Blue Ridge Summit PA 17214

8. Camping in Alaska

A camping vacation can be a rewarding and relatively inexpensive way to see the Great Land. Many people traveling the Alaska Highway to Alaska bring their own camping equipment, trailers, or motor homes, but there are also camper rental facilities in several cities for those who wish to fly up and then camp. There are a few extra things to consider while planning a camping vacation in Alaska, but with careful preparation and forethought, many potentially annoying or downright dangerous situations can be avoided.

The first consideration for many people is whether to bring a pet. Many people can and do bring their pets with them to Alaska, and this does not necessarily present any problem. Keep in mind, though, that pets must be kept on a leash at all government campgrounds within the state and are not allowed at all in national parks. There is a very good reason for this rule. Alaska is bear country; bears roam freely in every part of the state. Bears and dogs do not get along. The natural reaction of a dog threatened by a bear is to come running back to his master for protection, with the bear in hot pursuit. The easiest way to invite a confrontation with a bear is to have your dog along on a camping trip.

The next thing to consider is that you will be camping in bear country, which entails a few extra precautions on your part. The probability of being injured by a bear in Alaska is only about 1/50 that of being injured in an automobile accident on Alaskan highways, but with proper precautions, the probability drops much lower. It is legal in the state of Alaska to shoot a bear at any time of year in defense of life or property, but reasonable effort must be made to use means other than destruction of the animal. If it does become necessary to kill a bear, the hide of a black bear or the hide and skull of a brown bear must be immediately surrendered to the state.

The best protection against a bear is a high-powered rifle larger than 30.06, or a twelve-gauge shotgun loaded with either .00 buckshot or rifled slugs. A heavy pistol chambered for .357 magnum or larger is better than nothing, but the large-caliber rifle is considered best. Handguns are not

120

allowed in Canada, so pistols are out for those driving to Alaska. Also, guns of all types must be made inoperative before entering a national park, and shooting within the parks is not allowed.

It is helpful to understand certain elements of bear behavior and to know what to do if a confrontation does occur. When approached by a human at distances of fifty yards or more, a bear will often stand on its hind legs and swing its head to and fro. When a bear does this, he is trying to get a better idea of what you are. His eyesight is very poor, but his senses of smell and hearing are excellent, so help him out. Wave your arms over your head to help him see you, and talk to him in a firm tone of voice. Often, bears will move off once your identity is known to them. Bears often make a whoosh or woof sound as they turn to run when startled. As long as the bear runs, don't be alarmed. However, if a bear stands its ground and begins a *series* of woofs (like air being forced out of a bellows), or if it pops its teeth together, this is your invitation to leave. If the bear stands sideways and seems to stare off into space, it is showing you how big it is; this is also your invitation to leave. Leave slowly, facing the bear. *Never turn and run from a bear*. You *cannot* outrun him, and running may invite pursuit. If the bear follows you, drop or toss an article of clothing such as a hat for it to smell. Whatever you do, do not imitate a bear's sounds. If for some reason the bear actually gets ahold of you, lie still and don't move. The best position is on your stomach with your hands clasped over the back of your neck. Many men have lived to tell about a bear mauling by playing dead. A bear apparently isn't interested in you once he has "killed" you, and may even be repulsed by human odor.

Certain rules for camping reduce bear problems. When you select your campsite, pick a site away from animal trails. Leave strong-scented foods such as bacon and smoked fish at home, and avoid having scented cosmetics and soaps in your camp. You should separate your cooking area from your sleeping area for added protection. Store all food in plastic bags to seal in odors, and always store food away from camp in a tree if one is available. Never have any food in your tent. Wash your hands and face before getting in your sleeping bag. Don't bury anything. Burn or wash cans and foil to destroy odors. Collect garbage in a plastic bag, store it out of camp, and carry out everything that will not burn. Dump waste water away from your campsite.

When hiking, warn bears of your presence by making noises as you walk. Enter thickets from upwind so your smell will warn bears of your presence. Be aware of fresh bear signs such as tracks and droppings. If you detect the foul odor of decomposing meat while on the trail, stop. It's a cinch that a bear has already smelled it and is probably on the carcass or nearby. If you approach from upwind and don't smell it, you should recognize it by sight. Bears often cover their food with branches and forest

A trapper's cabin on the Petersville Road in the foothills of the Alaska Range. Moose antlers over the doorway signify to other residents that the owner has been successful in obtaining his meat for the winter season. Families will usually share their own meat with those who are not so fortunate, should the need arise.

litter after they've eaten their fill, then bed down nearby. If you see such a partially concealed cache, leave as quietly and quickly as possible.

The most popular months for camping are June through August, since these months are usually warmest, and all service facilities and camper parks are open during these months. Ferry reservations must be obtained well in advance since the ferries are usually booked solid during the peak summer season. May and September can also be delightful months to camp; campgrounds and lodges are not usually so crowded and ferry reservations are easier to obtain. Mosquitos and other insect pests are not so bothersome by the end of August. Most motels, campgrounds, and service stations along the highways remain open year-round, and regular, premium, and diesel gas is readily available. Along the more remote routes, however, some places do close down for the winter.

Some special attention should be given to motor homes, campers, and trailers before they are driven on gravel roads. Mud flaps are essential for pulling trailers and are very helpful to motor homes as well. They will prevent damage to the rear area of the vehicle, and the tires will throw less gravel at the people traveling behind. Many people like to protect the front of their camper or trailer (especially a front window) with plywood or hard plastic sheeting to protect it from flying gravel. Headlights do not break so often if protected with a clear plastic cover, which can be obtained inexpensively at almost any service station or garage along major highways.

Screened windows in campers are a necessary item to provide relief from flying insects. Two spare tires are recommended when traveling long gravel roads in remote areas, since tire repair facilities may be as much as fifty to one hundred miles away. Doughnut tires do not work well on gravel and should not be considered adequate as a spare. It is a good idea to have emergency items such as flares, flashlight, a small shovel, ice and bug scrapers, and a first aid kit along. In addition to emergency items, the following spare parts should be carried: trailer bearings, fan belts, jumper cables, plastic tape, siphon hose, wire, all-purpose glue, various-size rubber washers, sheet metal screws of various sizes, tire pump, air pressure gauge, tire repair kit, complete tool kit, points, condenser, spark plugs.

The speed limit is forty mph in Alaska for vehicles towing a trailer that exceeds eight feet in width. Also, vehicle and trailer combinations that exceed 10 feet in width, 13½ feet in height, or 65 feet in length need a special permit to travel Alaska roads. Trailers of the one-wheel castor type are unsatisfactory on all roads in Alaska and Canada, even the paved highways.

Safetywise, probably the most important thing to remember is to observe gross vehicle weight ratings to the letter and to make sure wheels and tires are of the proper size and properly inflated for the load being carried.

It is not necessary to carry along all the food and supplies you will need for the entire trip. These things are readily available along all highways and access roads in Alaska from May through October. Travel during the winter months, however, does require an emergency high-energy food supply and some items of special equipment for cold weather survival in case of breakdown in a remote area. These items should include extra wool blankets, a small portable stove, chemical hand warmers, fire extinguisher, shovel, ax, saw, waterproof matches, small pail, good hunting knife, baling wire, spare batteries for flashlights, and warning signals or flares. Tire chains should be carried, as they can be used for either snow or ice, and it is a good idea to have along extra gasoline.

There are almost unlimited camping opportunities within Alaska, from the most remote hike-in locations to the most sophisticated RV parks with full hookups, showers, and laundromats. It is possible to camp in locations accessible by canoes or rafts, places where bushplanes or floatplanes are the only means of access, and places accessible on horseback or by snowmachine. Remote cabins, maintained by the Forest Service within national forests, are available by reservation. One hundred forty-two cabins are located in the Tongass National Forest in southeast

Alaska and thirty-six in southcentral Alaska in the Chugach National Forest. Most of these cabins are accessible only by boat or plane, but a few can be reached over hiking trails. Most have oil or wood stoves, and all have tables and sleep six. Firewood is supplied by the Forest Service, but oil for oil stoves, bedding, and cooking utensils are the responsibility of the camper. There is no limit on the number of days that can be reserved, except for a three-day limit on hike-in cabins from May through August. Reservations must be specific as to the number of days and can be made up to 180 days in advance. The fee for use of these cabins is $10.00 per party per night.

There are no fees charged at Alaska state campgrounds and waysides; moderate fees (from $3.00 to $6.00) are charged by the U.S. Forest Service campgrounds located in the Tongass and Chugach national forests. There are about twenty-five camping areas in the state maintained by the Bureau of Land Management, and only one charges a fee. The National Park Service has seven campgrounds in Denali National Park. There are no fees charged at three of these, while the other four charge a fee of $6.00. The U.S. Fish and Wildlife Service also has several camping areas within the Kenai National Wildlife Refuge.

The following is a list of government campgrounds in Alaska, including those maintained by city governments. A list of privately operated campgrounds follows the government listings.

Government-Operated Campgrounds

Admiralty Island:

U.S. Forest Service Cabins
Admiralty Island National
  Monument
101 Egan Drive
Juneau AK 99801

Thirteen rustic cabins equipped with stoves at isolated locations on salt-water beaches and inland lakes. Boats provided at lake cabins. No electricity or plumbing.

Anchorage:

Alaska State Division of Parks
Director, Campgrounds
  System
619 Warehouse Ave.,
  Suite 210
Anchorage AK 99501

Public campgrounds throughout the state operated by the Alaska State Division of Parks. Information about all campgrounds is available on request.

Centennial Camper Park
Manager, Parks and Recrea-
    tion
Municipality of Anchorage
Pouch 6650
Anchorage AK 99502

Public campground with eighty-eight spaces operated by the city of Anchorage. Facilities include rest-rooms, showers, and firewood. There is a time limit of seven nights per season at all municipal camp-grounds in Anchorage.

Lion's Camper Park
Manager, Parks and Recrea-
    tion
Municipality of Anchorage
Pouch 6650
Anchorage AK 99502

Public campground with fifty spaces and ten tent sites at Russian Jack Springs. Campground has restrooms and showers, tennis courts, picnic areas, and hiking trails. There is also a pay telephone.

Chugach National Forest:

U.S. Forest Service Cabins
Anchorage District Ranger
Chugach National Forest
P.O. Box 10-469
Anchorage AK 99511

More than thirty cabins are main-tained in the Chugach National Forest. Each cabin has an oil or wood stove and rustic furniture but no electricity or plumbing. Some cabins are equipped with small boats.

U.S. Forest Service Camp-
    grounds
Chugach National Forest
2221 E. Northern Lights Blvd.
Anchorage AK 99508

Sixteen campgrounds are main-tained by the Forest Service. Each campground has water, sanitary facilities, tables, and fire grates. Two also have dump stations and flush toilets.

Cordova:

U.S. Forest Service Cabins
Cordova District Ranger
Chugach National Forest
P.O. Box 280
Cordova AK 99574

Fourteen cabins are in the Cordova district, some accessible by boat and some by hiking trails from the Copper River Highway. Skiffs pro-vided at cabins on Martin and Stump lakes. There is no plumbing or electricity.

Denali National Park Area:

Byers Lake Campground
Denali State Park
Box 182
Palmer AK 99645

Denali State Park campground located on the George Parks High-way, about ninety miles south of Denali National Park entrance. Strictly a wilderness park with no developed facilities.

Denali National Park & Pre-
serve
Superintendent
Box 9
McKinley Park AK 99755
Phone: (907) 683-2294

A total of seven campgrounds in
the park, four for RVs and one for
backpackers only. No advance reservations are accepted. Registration
for four limited access grounds can
be made on the day of arrival for
the length of stay—all others are on
a nightly basis.

Fairbanks:

Chatanika Campground
Alaska Division of Parks
4220 Airport Way
Fairbanks AK 99701

There are twenty-five spaces
located at mile 39, Steese Highway.
Facilities include restrooms, picnic
tables, fireplaces, and running
water. There is no fee at this campground. Closed in winter.

Chena River Recreation Area
Alaska Division of Parks
4220 Airport Way
Fairbanks AK 99701

There are restrooms and picnic
tables at this free campground
located on the Chena Hot Springs
road between mile 26 and 50. It is
open year-round.

Harding Lake Recreation Area
Alaska Division of Parks
4220 Airport Way
Fairbanks AK 99701

Eighty-nine spaces on the Richardson Highway at mile 42. There is
no fee at this campground. Facilities
include restrooms, picnic tables,
fireplaces, water, and dump station.

Haines:

Chilkat State Park
Haines Chamber of
Commerce
Box 518
Haines AK 99827

Thirty-three campsites seven miles
from Haines on Mud Bay Road.
Picnic shelter, boat launch, hiking
trail. Good sportfishing and no fees.
Good area to view bald eagles.

Chilkoot Lake
Haines Chamber of
Commerce
Box 518
Haines AK 99827

Thirty-two sites located at mile 10
Lutak Road, five miles beyond the
ferry terminal. Good fishing, boat
launch, and picnic shelter. Bald
eagles.

Mosquito Lake Wayside
Haines Chamber of
Commerce
Box 518
Haines AK 99827

Located at mile 13 Haines Highway, this thirteen-site campground
offers a picnic shelter, boat launch,
and good trout fishing.

Portage Cove Campgrounds
Haines Chamber of
  Commerce
Box 518
Haines AK 99827

Accessible to backpackers only;
located two miles south of Haines
on Lynn Canal Beach Road. There
are nine campsites, but no water is
available.

Juneau:

Auke Village Campground
U.S. Forest Service
Information Center
101 Egan Drive
Juneau AK 99801

Located at mile 15.8 Glacier Highway, this campground has eleven
campsites adjacent to saltwater
beaches. There is running water
with both pit and flush toilets.
Hiking, fishing, and boating are
available in the area.

Mendenhall Lake Camp-
  ground
U.S. Forest Service
Information Center
101 Egan Drive
Juneau AK 99801

This campground has sixty sites and
affords a beautiful view of Mendenhall Glacier. There are both pull-
through and drive-in slots with pit
toilets, running water, and dump
station. No reservations taken at
federal campgrounds.

Katmai National Park:

Brooks River Campground
Katmai National Park & Pre-
  serve
P.O. Box 7
King Salmon AK 99613

Located on the shore of Naknek
Lake about ¼ mile from Brooks
Lodge, this campground offers ten
sites for tents. Three sites have
wood shelters. Tables, toilets, and
food cache.

Kenai Peninsula:

Captain Cook State Park
Kenai Chamber of Commerce
Box 497
Kenai AK 99611

There are three campgrounds
within this state park: Discovery
Campground, fifty-seven units;
Stormy Lake ten units; and Bishop
Creek, twelve tent spaces. All have
water and toilets.

Kenai Municipal Park
Kenai Chamber of Commerce
Box 497
Kenai AK 99611

This camper park offers running
water, picnic shelters, restrooms,
and fireplaces. Activities in the area
include sportfishing, boating, and
beachcombing.

Ketchikan:

Ward Lake Recreation Area
U.S. Forest Service
313 Federal Building
Ketchikan AK 99901

Three public-use campgrounds in
this area have a total of fifty-three
units. Signal Creek, Settler's Cove,
and Last Chance campgrounds are
available for RVs. Three C's is for
backpackers only. All have firewood, toilets, and water.

Klawock:

Klawock Camper/Trailer
    Court
Box 113
Klawock AK 99925

City-maintained eighteen-unit
camper park in the city of Klawock.
Facilities include water and a dump
station.

Kodiak:

Buskin State Recreation Site
Kodiak District Super-
    intendent
Alaska Division of Parks
Box 3800
Kodiak AK 99615

Eighteen RV campsites with water,
restrooms, and a dump station. The
entire Kodiak National Wildlife
Refuge is open to camping, but
there are no other established
campgrounds in the area. The
Buskin Site has beach access and
fishing.

Public Use Cabins
Kodiak National Wildlife
    Refuge
Box 825
Kodiak AK 99615

There are twelve recreation cabins
in the Kodiak National Wildlife
Refuge maintained for public use.
All are equipped with stoves and
are accessible by either boat or
seaplane. Seven-day limit; first-
come, first-served.

Misty Fjords National Monument:

U.S. Forest Service Cabins
Tongass National Forest
313 Federal Building
Ketchikan AK 99901

Reservations may be made up to
six months in advance for these
rustic cabins about thirty-five miles
east of Ketchikan in Misty Fjords.
Access is by boat or floatplane.
Some cabins have boats.

Petersburg:

U.S. Forest Service Cabins
Petersburg Ranger District
P.O. Box 1328
Petersburg AK 99833

Twenty isolated cabins in the Petersburg area are equipped with wood or oil stoves and furniture. Reservations up to six months in advance. Some lake cabins have skiffs.

U.S. Forest Service Camp-
  grounds
Petersburg Ranger District
P.O. Box 1328
Petersburg AK 99833

This campground is located on Mitkof Island about twenty miles south of Petersburg. Pit toilets, fire-places, and picnic tables. No re-servations are accepted. No fee.

Seward:

U.S. Forest Service Cabins
Seward Ranger District
P.O. Box 275
Seward AK 99664

There are eleven cabins in remote locations near Seward. All cabins have stoves and furniture, but none has electricity or plumbing. Some lake cabins are equipped with boats.

U.S. Forest Service Camp-
  grounds
Seward Ranger District
P.O. Box 275
Seward AK 99664

Eight campgrounds with a total of 266 spaces are maintained by the Forest Service in the Seward area. All sites have water, toilets, tables, and fire grates.

Sitka:

U.S. Forest Service Cabins
Sitka Ranger District
Box 2097
Sitka AK 99835

Twenty wilderness cabins are located on Baranof, Chichagof and Kruzof Islands in the Sitka area. Access is by boat or floatplane from Sitka. Reservations up to six months in advance.

U.S. Forest Service Camp-
  grounds
Sitka Ranger District
Box 2097
Sitka AK 99835

Two campgrounds with a total of forty-seven campsites on the Sitka road system are suitable for tents, trailers, and campers. Two-week maximum at Starrigavan Bay and one month at Sawmill Creek.

Skagway:

Hanousek Park
Skagway Chamber of
   Commerce
P.O. Box 194
Skagway AK 99840

Fifty-space campground owned and operated by the city of Skagway. Facilities include dump station, toilets, and electrical hookups. Park located at corner of 14th and Broadway.

Tongass National Forest:

U.S. Forest Service
Regional Forester
Centennial Hall
101 Egan Drive
Juneau AK 99801

There are 144 Forest Service cabins in remote locations throughout the Tongass National Forest. Detailed information, including a map of the forest (which includes most of southeast Alaska) will be sent on request.

Wrangell:

U.S. Forest Service Cabins
Wrangell District Ranger
Box 51
Wrangell AK 99929

There are twenty-one remotely located cabins in the district, some with small boats. All have oil or wood stoves and rustic furniture. Reservations may be made up to six months in advance.

Yakutat:

U.S. Forest Service Cabins
Yakutat Work Center
Box 327
Yakutat AK 99689

Fourteen cabins are in the Yakutat area, some accessible by the Yakutat road system. Others may be reached over hiking trails or by aircraft or boat. Reservations six months in advance.

Private Campgrounds

Anchorage:

Golden Nuggett RV Park
Malaspina Properties
4100 DeBarr
Anchorage AK 99508

Eighty-six RV spaces with complete hook-ups. Paved campground near downtown Anchorage with free showers, playground, and laundry facilities.

Green Belt Camper Park
5550 Old Seward Highway
Anchorage AK 99502

Sixty spaces with full hook-ups, showers, and laundromat. Convenient to office locations and hospitals. Open year-round.

Highlander Camper Park
Executive Motel
2704 Fairbanks Street
Anchorage AK 99503

Forty spaces with hook-ups, no reservations needed. Restaurant and bar. Reasonable rates. Motel units adjoining feature kitchenettes and one to four beds per room.

Johnson Camper Park
3543 Mt. View Drive
Anchorage AK 99504

Forty-three camper spaces with full hook-ups, hot showers, dump station, and bathroom facilities. Motel with kitchenettes adjoins camper park.

Panoramic View Camper Park
Star Route A, Box 3500-A
Anchorage AK 99502

Located at the corner of the New Seward Highway and Huffman Road, this 115-space camper park has showers, laundromat, and garbage disposal.

Delta Junction:

Bergstad's Travel Park
Sigurd Bergstad
Box 273
Delta Junction AK 99737

One hundred five pull-through camper sites with full hook-ups at mile 1421 Alaska Highway in Delta Junction. Facilities include car wash, laundry, dump, showers, and propane. Wooded tent sites nearby.

Windy Court
Elizabeth Wallace
Box 454
Delta Junction AK 99737

Located at mile 192 Richardson Highway, this twenty-space camper facility features full hook-ups, water, sewer, propane, and dump station. Member of Good Sam Club with store and laundromat.

Denali National Park Area:

McKinley KOA Kampground
Manager
Box 34
Healy AK 99743

Full facility campground at mile 248.5 Parks Highway, ten miles north of Denali National Park. Nightly recreation, picnic tables and fireplaces, dog runs, auto repair, groceries and ice. Hook-ups, laundry, and transportation to and from park.

Fairbanks:

Chena Hot Springs
1919 Lathrop St., Drawer 25
Fairbanks AK 99701

Unlimited spaces at mile 56 Chena Hot Springs, but no hook-ups. Water, fireplaces, picnic tables, showers, restrooms accessible to handicapped.

Long Creek Lodge
529 Fifth Avenue
Fairbanks AK 99701

Campground with showers, laundromat, bar, dump station, and general store.

Monson Motel Campgrounds
1321 Karen Way
Fairbanks AK 99701

Thirty hook-ups, ten minutes from downtown Fairbanks. Facilities include restrooms, showers, dump station, and laundry room.

Nenana Public Campground
Mile 305 Parks Highway
Nenana AK 99760

No fee at this campground located at mile 305 George Parks Highway. There are restrooms, fireplaces, and handicapped facilities. Pets welcome.

Norlite Campground, Inc.
1660 Pegger Road
Fairbanks AK 99701

Camper park has 250 spaces for campers, tents, and trailers. Car wash, restrooms, and showers. Hook-ups, laundry, liquor, grocery, and dump.

Rainbow Valley RV Court
Star Route Box 50216
Fairbanks AK 99701

Eighteen spaces with hook-ups located at the corner of the Steese Highway and Chena Hot Springs Road. Water, showers, restrooms. Closed in winter.

Santa Claus House
Mile 12 Richardson Highway
North Pole AK 99705

Twenty-five units with no fee located twelve miles from town. Water and picnic tables included in the facilities.

Tanana Valley Fairgrounds
Box 188
Fairbanks AK 99707

Thirty spaces with fireplaces, firewood, picnic tables, dumping station, and coin laundry. Modern restrooms and showers. Closed in winter.

Tumwater Lake Lodge
   and Summer Shades Campground
Mile 290 Parks Highway
Nenana AK 99760

Lodge and campground located on five-acre lake for swimming and boating. Fishing and hunting licenses and supplies, store, gift shop, cabins. Campground has laundry and showers, and sells oil, gas, and propane.

Glennallen:

Tolsona Wilderness
  Campground
Box 23
Glennallen AK 99588

Campground at mile 173 Glenn Highway has fifty spaces with trees; each space fronts on river. Restrooms, showers, and dump station. Sportfishing for grayling.

Haines:

Eagles Nest Campground
Gwen Horton
Box 267
Haines AK 99827

Located at mile ½ Haines Highway, this campground has twenty spaces with water, sewer, and electrical hook-ups. Eight more spaces have only electricity. Geared for self-contained units.

Port Chilkoot Camper Park
Box 473
Haines AK 99827

Forty RV spaces and wooded area for tents. Hotel nearby. Facilities include showers and laundry room.

Homer:

Homer Spit Campground
John and Peggy Chapple
Box 1196
Homer AK 99603

Located at mile 181 Sterling Highway on the Homer Spit, this facility offers space for RVs and tents, with playground, fishing gear rentals, and bait. Showers, restrooms, tables, and fireplaces.

Juneau:

Tides Camper Park
5000 Glacier Hwy, Suite 1
Juneau AK 99801

Thirty-eight spaces with water and electricity. Facilities include bathrooms, showers, and laundry. Convenient to Mendenhall Glacier.

Kenai Peninsula:

Brown's Sportsmen's Service
Harry Warren
Box 256, Star Rt. 2
Sterling AK 99672

Located at mile 81 Sterling Highway, this camper park offers spaces with full hook-ups or electric only. Laundry facilities, general store, dump station, and showers. Guided fishing tours.

M & A Acres
Michael G. Wiley
Box 83
Clam Gulch AK 99568

Private homestead that caters to self-contained motor homes. Clam-digging, sportfishing and good opportunities for photography. Alaskan barbeque weekly on request.

Pedersen's Moose River
  Resort
Box 223, Star Rt. 2
Sterling AK 99672

This resort features canoes, boats, tackle, and a miniature golf course. Four cabins are available in addition to campgrounds. Showers and snack shop.

Sunrise KOA Campground
5117 Shorecrest Drive
Anchorage AK 99515
Phone (907) 243-4470

Located 7½ miles off Seward Highway on the Hope Road. Gold panning and fishing for salmon and trout on famed Six Mile Creek. Showers, laundry, store, and ice. Full hook-ups and propane sales.

Matanuska Glacier:

Glacier Park Resort
John H. Kimball
Box 4-2615
Anchorage AK 99509

Ten spaces with RV hook-ups and secluded campsites for tents. Cabins and rooms with baths available. Easy walk or drive to face of glacier. Laundry, showers, dump, propane, gift shop, and liquor store.

Palmer/Willow:

Barry's Resort
Box 1792
Palmer AK 99645

Forty RV spaces, restaurant, and lounge. Sportfishing for salmon and rainbow trout. Boat rentals, liquor store, and gas station.

Eklutna Lodge
Troy Jones
Star Route
Chugiak AK 99567

Ten-unit motel and thirty-six-unit camper park located twenty-six miles east of Anchorage on the Glenn Highway. Banquet room with dance floor, liquor store, grocery and laundromat. Hot showers and sanitary dump.

Green Ridge Camper Park
Star Route, Box 5031
Wasilla AK 99687

Full hook-ups for thirty-five camper spaces. Laundry facilities.

Matanuska Lake Park
Star Route A
Box 6157
Palmer AK 99645

Campground with picnic area located at the junction of the Glenn and Parks highways. Activities include horseback riding, swimming, hiking, boating, fishing, and bicycling. Horse rental available.

Montana Creek Lodge
Star Route A, Box 560
Willow AK 99688

Twenty-five camper sites at mile 96.5 George Parks Highway, but no hook-ups. Cabins are available. Bar and restaurant, showers, restrooms, and propane sales.

Nancy Lake Marina
Manager
Box 114
Willow AK 99688

Twenty-six camping spaces and cabins for rent. Restrooms and showers, boat and motor rentals, and snowmachine rentals. Store with fishing tackle and fuel. Summer sternwheeler tours and winter cross-country skiing.

Sheep Mountain Lodge
Star Route C, Box 8490
Palmer AK 99645

Twelve camper/trailer sites at mile 113.5 Glenn Highway. Laundromat with hot showers, sauna, and hot tub. Cabins and trailer unit also available.

Tok:

Golden Bear Motel
Box 276
Tok AK 99780

Twenty-seven pull-through trailer hook-ups and space for tent and and camper sites. Laundry, picnic area, free Alaska movies, gift shop, and wildlife display.

Sourdough Campground
Ted Timmons
Box 47
Tok AK 99780

Tent sites and pull-through sites for trailers separated by birch and spruce trees. Full hook-ups. Restrooms, hot showers, car wash, laundromat, and dump station. 1½ miles south of Tok.

Tundra Lodge
KOA Campground
Box 336
Tok AK 99780

Located at mile 1315 Alaska Highway. Park has fifty-four trailer and RV hook-ups, and spaces for tents with fireplaces and picnic tables. Showers, car wash, laundry, restaurant, lounge, groceries, and gifts.

9. Floating Alaska's Rivers

In Alaska it is possible to float thousands of miles on the river systems, lakes, and sheltered seaways by boat, canoe, raft, or kayak. The rivers range from peaceful fishing waters and canoe trails to whitewater too dangerous for even the journeyman river runner to negotiate; from areas of simple and uncomplicated access to areas where access is unusually expensive and difficult. Some rivers have characteristically bad weather, requiring patience in arranging a put-in and take-out point; others may be runnable for only a relatively short period of time each summer.

Waters in the Arctic can be cold. Although there are no glacial rivers large enough for boating in the Arctic, water temperatures range from the low thirties to the low sixties. Permafrost, permanently frozen ground, is virtually continuous in this area, and melting winter snows and summer rains can cause water levels to rise rapidly since water cannot penetrate very deeply into the soil. Periods of dry weather can also cause the water level to drop just as dramatically.

The best season for river running depends upon the area of the state in which the river is located and the elevation at which the trip is to commence. Most rivers in the southern part of Alaska can be successfully negotiated by late May or June through late August or September, while some rivers in the north can be run only during July and August. This limited season is mainly due to the fact that some rivers, especially in the Brooks Range, require access by floatplane to headwater lakes, which are generally ice-free later than the rivers themselves.

Because of the low water temperatures, life preservers are mandatory. A small camp stove is recommended gear as well, since in tundra areas firewood may not be readily available for campfires. Sandy gravelbars are the preferred camping site, since they offer flat, convenient, comfortable tent sites, a plentiful supply of firewood (in areas that do have trees), and often a gentle breeze to keep the bugs at bay. Also, these areas are regularly cleaned by nature during high-water periods, washing away any traces of civilization which may be left behind.

Normally, the least expensive method of access to areas without roads is to fly on regularly scheduled commercial airlines to the town closest to the put-in point, then charter the remaining distance. Similarly, the least expensive take-out normally involves ending the river trip at a village with scheduled commercial service. Scheduled commercial service to small communities in Alaska is often provided by small aircraft with limited seating and baggage capacities, so it is wise to let the carrier know your requirements ahead of time. Air carriers to small communities frequently substitute larger capacity aircraft if the demand is sufficient and known in advance for a specific flight.

There are several areas in the state where canoe and river trails have been established. There is an elaborate system of canoe trails on the Kenai Peninsula, where the Swan Lake and Swanson River systems offer miles of mapped trails with numerous portages and access points. Information on these trails can be obtained by writing to:

> Kenai National Wildlife Refuge
> P.O. Box 2139
> Soldotna AK 99669

The Nancy Lake Recreation area north of Anchorage has a major lake trail that connects the twenty-some lakes and ponds in the area. In addition, there are about 100 other lakes and ponds suitable for boats and canoes in the surrounding countryside. For information on this system write to:

> Alaska Division of Parks
> Superintendent, Mat-Su District
> Box 182
> Palmer AK 99645

Established river trail systems near both Anchorage and Fairbanks are managed by the Bureau of Land Management. Brochures on these trails are available and include portages, access points, degree of difficulty, and other helpful information. They can be obtained by writing:

> Bureau of Land Management
> Box 1150
> Fairbanks AK 99701

Lakes, rivers, and sheltered seaways within national forests, parks, monuments, preserves, and wildlife refuges provide unlimited opportunities for boating. Most of these rivers are in areas that are not accessible by road, so special consideration must be given to put-in and take-out points. Inflatable rafts or folding canvas or rubber kayaks are usually easier (and less expensive) to fly in by plane. Information on rivers and river running within national areas can be obtained by contacting the appropriate federal agency in charge at the following addresses:

National Park Service
2525 Gambell St., #107
Anchorage AK 99503

U.S. Fish & Wildlife Service
1011 E. Tudor Road
Anchorage AK 99503

Bureau of Land Management
P.O. Box 13
Anchorage AK 99513

The Alaska National Interest Lands Conservation Act has given wild and scenic river classification to twenty-three different rivers and streams in Alaska and is considering this classification for twelve others. There are three categories under the Wild and Scenic Rivers Act. The "wild" classification preserves the wilderness aspect of the rivers; no development is ever planned for these areas. The "scenic" classification permits some development, and the "recreational" classification is the least restrictive of the three. There are thirteen of these rivers within the national park system, six in the national wildlife refuge system, and two in conservation areas managed by the Bureau of Land Management. The remaining five rivers lie outside any designated preservation units.

Rivers Within National Park Areas:

Alagnak	Katmai National Preserve
Alatna	Gates of the Arctic National Park and Preserve
Aniakchak	Aniakchak National Monument
	Aniakchak National Preserve
Charley	Yukon-Charley Rivers National Preserve
Chilikadrotna	Lake Clark National Park and Preserve
John	Gates of the Arctic National Park and Preserve
Kobuk	Gates of the Arctic National Park and Preserve
Koyukuk (North Fork)	Gates of the Arctic National Park
Mulchatna	Lake Clark National Park and Preserve
Noatak	Gates of the Artic National Park and Noatak National Preserve
Salmon	Kobuk Valley National Park
Tinayguk	Gates of the Arctic National Park and Preserve

Rivers Within National Wildlife Refuges:

Andreafsky	Yukon Delta National Wildlife Refuge
Ivishak	Arctic National Wildlife Refuge

Nowitna	Nowitna National Wildlife Refuge
Selawik	Selawik National Wildlife Refuge
Sheenjek	Arctic National Wildlife Refuge
Wind	Arctic National Wildlife Refuge

Rivers Within Bureau of Land Management Units:

Beaver Creek	White Mountains National Recreation Area
	Yukon Flats National Wildlife Refuge
Birch Creek	Steese National Conservation Area

Rivers Outside Designated Preservation Units:

Alagnak	Outside and west of Katmai National Park and Preserve
Delta River	Tangle Lakes area to a point ½ mile north of Black Rapids
Fortymile River	Main stem and tributaries
Gulkana River	From Paxson Lake to Sourdough Creek
Unalakleet River	About 65 miles of the main stem

Rivers Designated for Study:

Colville River	Koyuk River	Situk River
Etivluk-Nigu Rivers	Melozitna River	Squirrel River
Kanektok River	Porcupine River	Utukok River
Kisaralik River	Sheenjek River	Yukon River

Rental boats can be somewhat difficult to find in Alaska. The larger cities usually have rental shops and some outfitting outlets. There are also organizations and individuals who offer a variety of still- and whitewater trips on Alaska's rivers, lakes, and streams, lasting from one day to several weeks. Many such trips combine river touring with excellent opportunities to sportfish and camp, and many operators furnish complete gear, including food. A listing of River Tour operators follows.

River Guides and Outfitters

Statewide:

Alaska Float Trips
Box 8264
Anchorage AK 99508

Provides guided canoe and raft trips throughout Alaska. Group size generally limited to ten.

Alaska Travel Adventures
200 North Franklin Street
Juneau AK 99801

Ten scheduled river expeditions in
Alaska and the Yukon. Also custom
guided trips. Canoe, kayak, or raft
on calm or whitewater.

Alaska Wilderness River Trips
John Ginsburg
Box 1143
Eagle River AK 99577

Guided wilderness river float trips
in central, southwest, and far north
Alaska. Rates include bush flights,
meals, equipment and personnel.

Alaska Wilderness Unlimited
Box 4-2477
Anchorage AK 99509

Guided wilderness river photography trips on wide range of rivers.
Rates include flying, meals, and
rafts or kayaks.

Arcticsport: Expeditions North
Box 1886
Anchorage AK 99510

Whitewater and wilderness float
trips and guided and unguided
backpacking trips. Good sportfishing and photography.

Far North Journeys
Jim Anderson/Celia Denny
Box 959
Anchorage AK 99510

Choice of scheduled or custom
trips by canoe, raft, or on foot.
Water and wilderness in all parts of
Alaska. Rates include guides, equipment, and meals. Groups of twelve.

Far North Ski Guides, Inc.
David R. Scott
Box 995 Glacier Valley
Girdwood AK 99587

Custom river trips throughout the
summer and winter helicopter ski
packages. Length ranges from five
days to several weeks. Camping
equipment available.

Fishing Float Trips
Fishing International
4000 Montgomery Drive
Santa Rosa CA 95405

Fully guided float trips through
spectacular wilderness for sportfishing. Rainbow trout, char, grayling,
and salmon. Custom trips range
from three to seven days.

Goldsteam Expeditions of
   Alaska
John Addis
Star Route 20194
Fairbanks AK 99701

Backpacking, skiing, sportfishing,
canoeing, kayaking, dogsledding
and photo safaris via guided and
unguided whitewater expeditions.
All areas, any length trip.

Hugh Glass Backpacking
   Company
Chuck Ash
Box 10-796
Anchorage AK 99511

Scheduled and custom trips anywhere in the state for hiking,
canoeing, kayaking, fishing, and
photography. Outfitting included.
Certified river and wilderness guide.

Weber-Alyeska Wilderness
 Guides
Sepp Weber
Box 10-1663
Anchorage AK 99511

River touring by raft, canoe, and kayak. Also hiking and ski touring. Raft, canoe, and kayak rental. Bilingual: English and German.

Southeast:

Alaska Discovery, Inc.
Wilderness Adventures
Box 26
Gustavus AK 99826

Canoe, kayak, and backpacking trips to Glacier Bay, Admiralty Island, Tracy Arm, Russell Fjord and other areas. Complete outfitting services.

Alaska Rivers
D.J. Mackay, Outfitter
Box 7575
Salt Lake City UT 84107

Wild and scenic river expeditions in all areas of Alaska. Ten- to twenty-day trips on Noatak, Tatshenshini, Copper, Susitna, and others. Southeast, Arctic, Coastal, and Central.

Chilkat Guides
Box G
Haines AK 99827

River trips in and around Glacier Bay and the St. Elias Mountains. Includes Alsek-Tatshenshini, Chil-kat, and Tsirku rivers.

Glacier Country River Trips
Mark Jensen
Box G
Haines AK 99827

Rafting trips on the Tsirku River near Glacier Bay; includes flight to cabin put-in point. One-day float trip on Chilkat includes lunch.

Juneau Airboat Charters
Bill & Kathy Brown
Box 2869
Juneau AK 99803

Daily wilderness expeditions on Berner's Bay river systems in Tongass National Forest. Includes transportation, rain gear, and lunch. Fishing equipment available.

Mountain Guides, Inc.
Box 911
Wrangell AK 99929

Guided or unguided Stikine River raft trips. Boat charters around Wrangell Island and to Anan Bay to watch bears fishing for salmon.

Stikine River Adventures
Chuck Traylor
Box 1380
Wrangell AK 99929

One- to five-day Stikine River tours in twenty-five-foot aluminum craft. Day tours include LeConte Glacier. Five-day tours include all gear but sleeping bags and personal gear.

Travelot Travel Agency
P.O. Box 288
Haines AK 99827

River rafting daily on Chilkat River at Haines. Guided two- to three-day raft trips on the Tsirku River. Reservations needed.

Wrangell Charters
Box 1062
Wrangell AK 99929

Stikine River trips in boats up to sixty-five feet. Any length tour. Combine hot springs baths, fishing, and photography.

Southcentral:

Adventure River Company
P.O. Box 35
Talkeetna AK 99676

Five-, seven-, and twelve-day packages on Copper, Susitna, Noatak, and the east fork of the Chandalar River. Maximum of twelve.

Alaska Campout Adventures
Bill Wright
6458 Citadel Lane
Anchorage AK 99504

Seven- and ten-day floatfishing trips with guides and food, lodging, and equipment. Also daily rafting on Kenai River. Two- and four-day campouts. Statewide trips.

Alaska Mountain Treks
Star Route 10363B
Fairbanks AK 99701

Small personalized expeditions in the Brooks, Alaska, and Aleutian ranges on wild rivers in remote areas.

Alaska Pioneer Canoers
  Association
Box 931
Soldotna AK 99669

Guided sportfishing and canoe trips on the Kenai Peninsula. Rental boats available.

Alaska River and Ski Tours,
  Ltd.
George Heim or Carl Dixon
1801 Sunrise Drive
Anchorage AK 99504

Two- to ten-day float trips in the Bristol Bay area and ten-day trips on the Copper River. All rafts and equipment provided. Sportfishing.

Alaska River Expeditions
Star Route Box 5086
Wasilla AK 99687

Custom jetboat trips on the Yukon, Susitna, Chandalar, and Porcupine rivers. Experience the wilderness.

Alaska River Touring
  Company
Dan Gabryszak
P.O. Box 1884
Anchorage AK 99504

Various length float trips on the Yukon, Matanuska, Kenai, and Deshka rivers. Also any other navigable river in Alaska with sixty-day notice.

Beluga Wilderness Outfitters
Gerald Yeiter
Star Route A, Box 81-Y
Anchorage AK 99507

Three- to seven-day float trips personalized to fit needs. Sportfishing, hunting, photography. Fly-in/drop off program with guide. Base at main lodge.

Denali Waterways
Summit Lake Lodge
Delta Junction AK 99737

Guided raft and canoe trips from tent camps in southcentral wilderness. Fishing, wildlife photography.

Denali Wilderness Treks
Keith Nyitray
Box 84
Talkeetna AK 99676

Meals, lodgings, river rafting, mountain expeditions, glacial ski touring, dogsledding, cross-country skiing, and wilderness backpacking. Day or week.

The Great Alaska River
    Company
Box 1440
Homer AK 99603

Kenai River whitewater raft trips for from four to twenty people. Day or overnight with certified guide. Fishing.

Kenai Canyon Float Trips
Bill Wright
6458 Citadel Lane
Anchorage AK 99504

Six-hour raft trips on Class 4 rapids in Kenai Canyon. Also two- and four-day overnight campouts. Statewide trips from basecamps for wilderness fishing.

Mahay's Talkeetna Riverboat
    Service
Box 113
Talkeetna AK 99676

Two sportfishing canyon tours on twenty-three-foot jet riverboat that are fully guided. Camping and fishing rentals.

Nova Riverunners of Alaska,
    Inc.
Box 444
Eagle River AK 99577

Features varied-length trips on the Matanuska, Chickaloon, Copper, Kobuk and Noatak rivers. Arctic river specialists.

Portage River Adventures
Box 260
Girdwood/Alyeska AK 99587

Variety of scenic float trips for up to fifty people. Season starts May 15 and ends September 15.

Open Door Alaskan Water
    Adventures
Kari Becker
Box 1185
Cordova AK 99574

Marine kayak and whale-watching trips in Prince William Sound for six to sixteen days. Copper River raft trips with multilingual guides. Food and gear.

River Riders, Inc.
2111 Chandalar Drive
Anchorage AK 99504

One- to six-day whitewater raft trips for up to fourteen people. All food, transportation, and overnight camping gear.

Silvertip Float Trip
  Adventures
Box 6389
Anchorage AK 99502

Fully guided float and sportfishing
trips on the Chulatna and
Talachulitna rivers.

Interior and Far North:

Alaska Fish and Trails Un-
  limited
Star Route Box 20154
Fairbanks AK 99701

Koyukuk River rafting and backpacking in the Brooks Range for
maximum of ten people. Guided
and unguided.

Alaska Raft Adventures
Box 427
Denali Nat. Park AK 99755

Guided wilderness float trips on
wide range of Alaska rivers including the Alagnak, Charley, and
Kobuk.

Alaska River Expeditions
Mark Jensen
Box G
Haines AK 99827

Raft trips on four rivers in the
Brooks Range. Also twelve-day trips
on Tatshenshini and Alsek rivers in
the St. Elias Mountains. Fare includes return to Haines.

Alaska Wilderness Adventures
Box 3
Kotzebue AK 99752

Guided float trips on the Kobuk
and Noatak rivers. Also combination hiking and photography trips.

The Arctic Guide Assocation
Bettles AK 99726

Wilderness trips on many Alaska
rivers including the John, Alatna,
Kobuk, Noatak, and Killik. Custom
trips.

Arctic Treks
Box 73452
Fairbanks AK 99707

Backpacking and rafting in the
Brooks Range and camping and
hiking in Gates of the Arctic. Certified guides.

Brooks Range Expedition
John Musser
Bettles Field AK 99726

Customized raft, canoe, or foldboat
trips in Central Brooks Range or in
Arctic National Wildlife Refuge.

Circle North River Trips
Roger Dowding
Circle AK 99733

Unguided float trips on the Yukon,
Porcupine, Kandik, and Charley
rivers. Eagle-to-Circle trips a
specialty.

General Bullmoose Canoe
  Tours
Star Route 30074
Fairbanks AK 99701

Canoe trips on the scenic rivers in
the Fairbanks area. All trips guided.
Three to four days with overnights,
or daily.

Kobuk River Company
Robin Sandvik
Box 2
Kiana AK 99749

Day tours of Kiana and surrounding area or river excursions to cabins along the Kobuk. Lodging, meals, and transportation provided. Good fishing.

R & L Enterprises
Ron Liewer
Box 86
Tok AK 99780

Raft and canoe trips on the Fortymile River from two to five days, longest from Chicken to Eagle. Package includes food, tents, boats, and shuttle service.

Rivers Unlimited
Jon Breivogel
Star Route Box 106
Copper Center AK 99573

Various tours, including one through huge hydraulics and whirlpools in Wood Canyon and then to face of glaciers near Million Dollar Bridge.

Ruby Roadhouse
Jim Hart
Box 6
Ruby AK 99768

Canoe, raft, or riverboat tours arranged on Melozitna, Yukon, Nowitna or Yuki rivers. Nowitna National Wildlife and hot springs nearby.

Sourdough Outfitters
Box 18
Bettles AK 99726

Outfitting for Central Brooks Range river trips. Specialty is Noatak River. Canoe rentals and riverboat charters.

Tatonduk Outfitters, Ltd.
P.O. Box 55
Eagle AK 99738

Yukon, Charley, Porcupine and Fortymile river raft trips arranged. From four to six people.

Southwest:

Alaska Fishing Adventures
1334 Bennister Drive
Anchorage AK 99504

Bristol Bay area float trips to Wood-Tikchik State Park. Rugged wilderness camping with no modern conveniences.

Alaska River Safaris
Ron Hyde
4909 Rollins Drive
Anchorage AK 99504

Deluxe heated tent camps in Togiak National Wildlife Refuge. Sportfishing by float trips to inaccessible areas. Four to six per guide and two per boat.

Alaska West River Tours
Box 24
Aleknagik AK 99555

Canoe or raft float trips from Bering Sea to Dillingham. Trophy fishing in entire area. Experienced guide.

Alaskan Sea Adventures
Bill G. Herman
P.O. Box 2225
Kodiak AK 99615

Ocean kayaking trips in fjords and headlands of Kodiak area and Alaska Peninsula. Scheduled trips or charters. Classes offered for college credit.

Bill Martin's Fish Alaska
Royal Coachman Lodge
Box 1887
Anchorage AK 99510

Nuyakuk, Togiak and Nushagak river float trips for sportfishing. Accommodations at lodge at outlet of Tikchik Lakes on Nuyakuk River.

10. Wildlife, Fishing, and Hunting

Alaska's Wildlife

Alaska's vast size and large areas of wilderness have made it the ideal place for wildlife to flourish undisturbed over the years. The number and variety of Alaska's wildlife is tremendous in comparison to any other area of the United States.

Here, in majestic solitude, is found Nanook, the great white polar bear. These huge bears spend most of their time on pack ice in the Arctic Ocean, coming on land usually only to den and give birth. They are well insulated against the cold of the Arctic, for it is thought that their "white" hair is not white at all but colorless and hollow. If so, it acts somewhat like a solar collector to store heat.

In Alaska too is found the coastal brown bear, the largest of all living carnivorous animals, thought to be descended from the prehistoric cave bear of northern Europe. Of the same species as the grizzly, these coastal bears average a much larger size than their inland brothers and have been known to reach heights of eight to nine feet and weights of up to 1300 pounds.

The somewhat smaller interior brown bear is usually referred to as the grizzly. Now very scarce in the rest of the United States, grizzlies are found in Alaska in great numbers, ranging through nearly every part of the state.

Black bears are found in Alaska as well, and in several color phases, including the rare blue phase. Bears of this color phase are often called glacier bears. Black bears are found throughout Alaska except in the far north, the extreme west, and some coastal sections of Southwest and Southcentral.

The deer family is represented by several species in Alaska. The small, delicate Sitka blacktail deer is found throughout the coastal forests of Southeast and along the gulf coast further north, where there is dense

Top: *Alaska barren ground caribou alongside the Glenn Highway in southcentral Alaska. These were photographed in May, when the animals' antlers are not fully grown and are covered in velvet. The antlers grow to full size by late August or September, and the velvet is stripped off shortly before the rutting season.* Bottom: *Moose are a common sight along highways in Alaska, as this sign testifies.*

vegetation due to the high amount of rainfall. The moose takes over where the blacktail deer leaves off and ranges throughout much of the rest of the state, especially in southcentral and interior regions, where there are forests of white and black spruce, birch, alder, and willow. These huge animals often exceed 1600 pounds in weight and browse on willow, birch, aspen, grasses, and sedges. Further towards the Arctic where forests generally give way to tundra, great herds of caribou graze on lichens and other tundra plants, although smaller groups of these animals can, and often do, range much further south. Reindeer, the somewhat smaller domesticated version of the caribou, are confined mostly to western and northern Alaska, where they are herded by native Alaskans to provide food and income for the people. Roosevelt elk can be found on two islands in Alaska, Rasberry and Afognak, where they were transplanted in 1928 from the Olympic Peninsula in Washington State.

Alaska has great numbers of mountain goats and Dall sheep. They are found in high, rugged mountains and remote valleys but can also be observed from highways and in refuges where they are protected. (Binoculars are helpful in sheep country because even when the sheep are spotted from the highway, they are usually very high up on the cliffs and ledges and cannot be seen at close range.) Both of these species occur in Alaska in their white color phase, the Dall sheep with massive, curling horns in the male and smaller, slightly curled horns in the female. The goats have horns very like an antelope and usually have longer hair and a beard. Mountain goats are confined mostly to Southeast and the Chugach, Talkeetna, and Wrangell mountains of Southcentral. Dall sheep stay more in the interior region, where they feed on grasses and sedges, lichens, dryas, and willow shoots.

One of the largest wolf populations in the world is found in Alaska, where the colors of their coats range from snow white to jet black. They are well adapted to live in almost every area of the state and are found everywhere except the Bering Sea Islands, the Aleutian Islands, and some Southeast and Prince William Sound islands. The wolves travel in packs and eat deer, moose, caribou, mice, and lemmings. In Alaska, these animals are seldom seen by man unless a special effort is made to observe them. Opinion is divided on whether the wolf is a help or a hindrance to wildlife ecology in the state. There are those who believe that wolves are essential to the ecological balance because they cull weak and sick animals from the herds of moose and caribou and help keep the population in check. There are others who feel that wolves wreak wanton destruction, killing for the sheer joy of it, thereby taking food animals away from the people who rely on them for sustenance.

Of the two fox species found in Alaska, the red fox is the more widespread, occurring throughout most areas of the state. The coat of an

Alaskan red fox is often a beautiful golden color rather than the red seen in the lower forty-eight. The arctic fox occurs in two color phases in Alaska. The blue phase is found most often in the Aleutian and Pribilof islands, while the white phase is more often seen along the western and northern coastal areas. The arctic fox has also been introduced to several other areas of the state for fox farming.

The lynx is the only species of large cat found in Alaska. Similar to the bobcat in size, the lynx has a very short, dark tail, long tufts of hair in its ears, and great big furry feet, which function as showshoes in deep snow. Snowshoe hares are the primary prey of the lynx, which prefers to hunt mostly at night, although some forced daylight hunting occurs in summer because of the long hours of daylight. Lynx are found throughout Alaska except for a few islands along the southeast and southwest coasts.

Perhaps the most unusual animal found in Alaska is the musk-ox. Because musk-oxen are an easy animal to kill (when threatened, they form a circle, placing the calves inside for protection), they became extinct in Alaska in the 1850s. During the 1930s, a small herd was shipped from Greenland and introduced on Nunivak Island in the Bering Sea. The herd thrived, and parts of the herd have since been transplanted to several other areas. It is hoped that eventually the musk-ox will range over its entire former habitat. The total number of musk-oxen in Alaska at present is about 1000 animals. The fine, wool-like underhair of the musk-ox, called quiviut, is woven by natives into exquisitely fine garments and scarves. Each musk-ox produces up to five pounds of quiviut annually.

In 1928, a small number of American bison were transplanted from Montana to a place in Alaska near Delta Junction, where they have thrived. Buffalo are notorious for being able to get through fences when they want to, and the fields of grain in the Delta Junction area present an irresistible temptation to the herd, who often become a nuisance to local farmers. There are now close to 1000 animals in Alaska, and other herds have been started at Healy, Farewell, and near the Copper and Chitina rivers. Hunting of these animals is now permitted on a regular basis, but is regulated by lottery permit to keep the populations in correct proportion. The meat is very high in protein and tastes much like beef, although it has a somewhat heavier flavor and is slightly darker in color.

Smaller animals living in Alaska include the muskrat, beaver, squirrel, marten, weasel, mink, and wolverine. These animals are all found throughout most of the state and provide food for larger mammals and birds, as well as meat and fur for man.

Alaska's population of marine mammals is also impressive. In the north of Alaska, walrus, seal, and otter abound. Some islands have migrant populations of thousands of these animals, and the noise they make can be heard for miles. Some of the older walrus weigh as much as

4000 pounds, and they live to be thirty-five years old. Each summer, the world's largest population of northern fur seals gather at the Pribilof Islands in the Bering Sea. The otters are the clowns of the sea world, and are frequently found inland along rivers. The hides of the otter are very valuable, and sealskins and walrus hides are often used for clothing and as skin covers for boats used by native Alaskans.

Sea lions and ten species of whales are also included among Alaska's marine mammals. The great blue whale, the largest of all whales, and the endangered humpback and gray whale are found in Alaska, as is the white beluga and killer whale.

At present, the marine mammal population of Alaska is managed by the federal government rather than by the state, although the state is now going through the necessary steps to assume management. Under federal management, it is illegal for anyone other than an Alaska native to take marine mammals for any reason. Natives may take marine mammals for subsistence purposes or for making native articles of handicraft and clothing for sale. In anticipation of the transfer of management to the state, there are tag fees listed for walrus in the state's hunting regulations, but they will not apply until transfer of management to the state is complete. (The same rules also apply to polar bears, since they spend most of their lives on the ice in northern seas.)

Very few bird species remain in Alaska during the winter, but every spring, millions of migratory birds flock to Alaska, crowding the skies in search of nesting and breeding grounds. Thousands of ducks, brant, and geese come to take advantage of Alaska's river flats, lakes, and tundra ponds, and millions of seabirds nest in colonies on exposed sea cliffs along Alaska's coastline. Cranes, terns, and gulls are found in great numbers, and the state is home to colorful puffins, magnificent bald eagles, and the endangered peregrine falcon. Trumpeter swans, which were once thought near extinction, nest in Alaska and have now reached a population of about 8000. The Copper River Delta is the only known breeding ground of the rare Canada dusky goose.

Two species of birds that do make Alaska their year-round home are the raven and the state bird, the willow ptarmigan. Ptarmigan are found in inland areas and change color with the season, becoming snow-white in the winter and brown in the summer.

Sportfishing

Sportfishing in Alaska is world famous, with a tremendous variety of fishing excursions from which to choose. There are fishing lodges and charter yachts; there is riverboat fishing and even ice fishing. Hundreds of sportfishing packages are available from tour guides, through travel agencies, and simply through making local inquiries.

There are eleven sportfishing management areas in Alaska, and each region has its own seasons, bag limits, and legal means of capture. A sportfishing license is required of all persons sixteen years of age or older, except persons over sixty who have lived in Alaska for thirty consecutive years or more. In addition to a license, all anglers are required to purchase and carry a special $5.00 permit for king salmon or steelhead trout. Fishing licenses are available from any fish and game office and are sold in sporting goods stores and sportfishing camps. They are available by mail by writing to the Licensing Section, Alaska Department of Revenue, Fish and Game Division, 1111 West 8th Street, Juneau AK 99801.

Fees for fishing licenses are as follows:

Resident:	$10.00
Nonresident:	
3-day license	$10.00
14-day license	$20.00

A resident is anyone who has lived in the state for twelve consecutive months and has continuously maintained voting residence during that time.

The principal sportfishing species available in Alaska, a general idea of the seasons they are available, and the types of lures and bait that seem to work best are easier to discuss if we consider the state section by section.

Southeast

Saltwater Fishing:

Halibut — Common throughout the entire area from May to September, peaking in inside waters in late August. Preferred baits are octopus and herring. Fine catches are also made by jigging with large spoons. The large halibut exceed 100 pounds and can be dangerous in a small boat.

King Salmon — Available from mid-March to September. The best period is from mid-May to mid-June, when the big ones, up to about seventy pounds, are available. The preferred bait is trolled or drifted herring. The edges of reefs where they drop off into deep water are good places to try.

Pink Salmon — Available during July and August. Good spots are

Mountain Point and the mouth of Lunch Creek near Ketchikan. Also try Auke Bay and Lena Cove near Juneau.

Rockfish — These bottom-feeders are available throughout the season and can often turn a dull day into an interesting one. Any bait fished on the bottom in rocky areas will produce these fine-flavored fish. Fish deep, as they range down to 600 feet.

Sea-run Cutthroat and Dolly Varden — Available from May to October. Small spoons, flies, and eggs are preferred. The best locations are where creeks and streams enter salt water.

Silver Salmon — Available from July through September. The best month is August. Herring or large spoons are the favored bait, and flashers are frequently used for attraction. Coho usually run shallow but do not necessarily follow shorelines. These fish average twelve pounds but can exceed twenty pounds.

Freshwater Fishing:

Cutthroat and Dolly Varden — This combination of sportfish is found as year-round freshwater residents and also as a migratory species. The resident fish are available throughout the year. The size range is wide, with fish up to seven pounds reported. The sea-run trout and char are found in creeks and streams from April to early June and again from late July to November. The best fishing occurs during late August and September. Baits to try are eggs, flies, and spoons.

Eastern Brook and Rainbow Trout — These fish have been successfully stocked in selected waters through the area. Eastern Brook can be found in numbers in lake waters near Juneau, Sitka, and Ketchikan. Rainbows are found in lakes near Petersburg and Ketchikan and on lower Baranof Island. Eggs, spoons, flies, and shrimp are the favored baits.

Grayling — Southeast anglers now have grayling fishing available. The grayling were first stocked in 1962 and now are providing excellent fishing, with many fish attaining two pounds. Small flies, shrimp, and spinners are the way to take these sailfin beauties. The places to try are Antler Lake, Juneau; Beaver Lake, Sitka; and Big Goat, Manzoni and Snow lakes near Ketchikan.

Silver Salmon — Found in streams open to fish migrations throughout the area. They are available from August to early November, with the peak occurring in September. Bright, shiny spoons and flies are favored. Baranof Island at Port Banks is a very good stream, as are the Situk and Italio rivers at Yakutat.

Steelhead — Two separate runs of this trophy fish occur in Southeast. In lower Southeast a fall run (during September and peaking in October) enters creeks that have accessible lakes in the system. These fish remain all winter and offer excellent fishing. The Ketchikan and Yakutat areas are particularly good. A spring run enters the larger creeks throughout all of Southeast in April and peaks in May. Eggs are the preferred bait, with spoons and flies running a close second.

Copper River–Prince William Sound

Saltwater Fishing:

Chum Salmon — Available during July and August and are taken frequently while fishing for pinks and silvers.

Clams — Littleneck clams are available in most gravel-mud beaches in protected bays at half-tide in Valdez Arm and Prince William Sound. Razor clams are abundant in the beaches near Cordova.

Dolly Varden — Sea-run dollies can be found in most of Prince William Sound during salmon runs and during the fall. The best areas to fish are in the vicinity of creek and river mouths. These fish will bite on eggs, flies, and a variety of lures.

Halibut and other bottomfish — A large variety of bottomfish can be found throughout the Sound. Generally, small bays are the best areas to fish. Jigging with large lures and bait can be very rewarding.

King Salmon — The best catches of this trophy fish are made near Valdez and Cordova in late winter and early spring. Large trolling lures and herring make the best bait.

Pink Salmon — Excellent pink salmon fishing is found in Prince William Sound throughout the summer. This excellent fish will take a wide variety of lures. Favorites are golf tees and spoons.

Silver Salmon — Become available in late July and remain present through mid-September. Excellent fishing occurs in the bays adjacent to Valdez and Cordova. A boat is required for best results; charter boats are available. Spoons and herring are proven lures for this scrappy fish.

Freshwater Fishing:

Burbot — The best fishing for this unusual fish is during the winter months. Good catches can be made after freezeup in Lake Louise, and Susitna, Leila, Hudson, Crosswind, Paxson and Summit lakes. Pieces of whitefish or herring make excellent bait.

Cutthroat Trout — Occurs in some lakes in Prince William Sound. The best time is immediately after ice is out and again during the late fall. Eggs and small spoons work well. There are many fly-in fisheries in the Copper River Basin for rainbow trout, lake trout, and grayling.

Dolly Varden – The best dolly varden fishing is in the streams near Valdez and Cordova. These fish are not too particular about what bait they prefer; anything from eggs to lures should work.

Grayling – Grayling fishing is good in most small roadside streams along the Glenn and Richardson highways. The best time for fishing in these streams is May and June during breakup. When the water is muddy, eggs are the best bait. Later in the year flies and small lures work well. Lake fishing for grayling is good throughout the summer. The Gulkana River usually has excellent grayling fishing throughout the summer. There are several automobile access points as well as a number of foot trails leading to the river.

King Salmon – Available in fair numbers in the Gulkana and Klutina rivers during June and July.

Lake Trout – The best catches of lake trout are generally made immediately after ice breakup and just prior to freezing. Fishing for "lakers" is good in Louise, Susitna, Beaver, Dog, Paxson, Summit, Swede, Tanada, and Copper lakes. Several small roadside lakes along the Denali Highway offer good lake trout fishing for the shore angler. Deep trolling after the water warms up is the best way, using spoons, red-eyes, or Alaskan plugs.

Rainbow Trout – Good rainbow trout fishing can usually be found in roadside lakes such as Worthington, Blueberry, Sculpin, Buffalo, and Van.

Red Salmon – Excellent red salmon fishing is available during late June and July in the Gulkana and Klutina rivers. Fishing with flies (streamers) is very effective and furnishes considerable sport and enjoyment.

Silver Salmon – Good catches of migrant salmon are possible along the Copper River Highway in the fall. Landlocked silvers can be taken at Strelna Lake on the Chitina-McCarthy Road with flies and small spoons during summer and eggs during winter.

Cook Inlet–Matanuska Valley

Saltwater Fishing:

Cook Inlet, north of the Forelands, is not suited to successful sportfishing because of silt-laden waters. Strong currents and extreme tidal fluctuations also reduce sportfishing opportunities.

Freshwater Fishing:

Chum Salmon — Scattered sparingly throughout the streams of Cook Inlet from mid-July through mid-August. Anglers may tie into a chum salmon in such locations as Willow, Alexander, and Montana creeks while fishing for pinks or silvers. Preferred chum lures are similar to those used for silvers.

Dolly Varden — This white or pink-spotted relative of the lake trout is not abundant in most upper Cook Inlet tributaries. However, the rivers and creeks northwest of Tyonek produce some nice dollies, and they are occasionally seen during the summer in the Theodore, Chuit, and Talachulitna rivers. Effective lures are eggs, brightly colored lead head jigs, and small spinning lures.

Eulachon — Smelt, commonly called "hooligan," are slender but tasty little fish taken primarily by long-handled dip nets during the short May spawning run. Hooligan are abundant in Placer and Twentymile rivers near Portage.

Grayling — This coldwater beauty may be taken during late May and early June. For the fly-in angler, the upper reaches of Lake Creek, the Talachulitna River, and Coal Creek provide good grayling fishing for most of the May-through-September period. Salmon eggs are best in spring or during high water, while flies and spinners are best in summer and fall.

King Salmon — This highly prized sportfish, the largest of all Pacific salmon, enters upper Cook Inlet waters in early June. It can be caught on a variety of spinning lures, oakie drifters and cluster eggs.

Lake Trout — Shell Lake near Skwentna provides an excellent lake trout fishery for fly-in anglers who have small motor-propelled rafts for trolling. Medium-sized red and white spoons and blue-tinted minnow-type lures, trolled to thirty-foot depths and greater, provide the action these fish like.

Pink Salmon — Odd-numbered years usually offer poor to fair "humpy" fishing in the Cook Inlet area. Mid-July through mid-August is the best time to catch the pinks. Small daredevils and a No. 1 red and white Mepps are proven lures for these fish.

Rainbow Trout — From late May until September first the Deshka River and Alexander and Lake creeks offer the fly-in fisherman some of the finest rainbow fishing available in Cook Inlet. Highway fishing is available on eastside tributaries of the Susitna river such as Willow and Montana creeks. Cluster eggs and artificial spinning-type lures are definitely preferred.

Silver Salmon — These spectacular game fish enter the area in mid-July and remain until September. The peak occurs in August. Some excellent fishing takes place on the Deshka River, Lake and Alexander creeks, Chuit River, Talachulitna River, and Quig Creek. All of these streams are on the west side of the Susitna River and are accessible only by plane or boat. Silvers are also available in eastside tributaries of the Susitna River. These tributaries are accessible by car from the George Parks Highway. Tee spoons and Mepps spinners are the lures most frequently used, and cluster eggs are always a sure thing. Stocked landlocked silver salmon are also available in Echo, Victor, Lucille, and Finger lakes.

Kenai Peninsula

Saltwater Fishing:

Bottomfish — The principal species found in the rocky bays of the Kenai Peninsula are halibut, rockfish, red snapper, ling cod, greenling, and flounder. They are available throughout the season and are best caught by fishing bait or jigging large silver lures near the bottom. Lower Cook Inlet from Deep Creek south to Kachemak Bay offers good halibut fishing. Razor clams or herring fished on a sandy bottom work well. Resurrection Bay in the vicinity of Cheval and Rugged islands offers the best bet for rockfish.

Clams — Razor clams are sporadically abundant along the sandy beaches between the Kasilof River and Anchor Point. Roads at Clam Gulch and Deep Creek provide access to the beach. The most popular area is at Clam Gulch, twenty-two miles south of Soldotna. The tasty bivalves can be dug throughout the spring and summer on minus tides. At least a −3.0-foot tide is recommended for beaches further south around Deep Creek and Happy Valley. Hardshell clams can be taken along the southern beaches of Kachemak Bay. Cockles can also be found on the east side of the Homer Spit.

Dolly Varden — Available throughout Kachemak Bay from early spring through the fall, with peak catches during July and August. "Dollies" are caught by shore anglers on the Homer Spit and can be taken from most southside beaches and stream mouths.

King Salmon — Available in lower Cook Inlet from mid-May through late July. The best king salmon fishing occurs in that portion of the inlet located south of a marker situated one mile south of Deep Creek. Trolling of bright spoons and herring is the most popular method. The kings in this fishery are quite large, with many exceeding fifty pounds.

Pink Salmon—Found throughout Kachemak Bay at Homer in July and early August. Pinks can be caught by casting small lures from the Homer Spit and from many beaches on the south side of the bay. Pink salmon are also abundant in Resurrection Bay at Seward in even-numbered years during this same time period.

Silver Salmon—Angling available from the road system in three areas of the peninsula: (1) Resurrection Bay, Seward, where they become available in early June with the run peaking in mid-August and terminating in early September; (2) Kachemak Bay, Homer, where these fish are present primarily during August and taken from the shore in Mud Bay on high tides; (3) Cook Inlet, near the beach, from late July through August, between Cape Ninilchik and Anchor Point. Best results require a boat, with herring, spoons, or spinners trolled near the surface.

Freshwater Fishing:

Arctic Char—Occur in the lakes of the Swanson River drainage and are popular with winter fishermen. They are also taken during the spring and fall. Warmer summer waters restrict these fish to cool depths, where they can be taken by deep trolling. Salmon eggs, spoons, and spinners are suggested baits.

Arctic Grayling—This species has limited distribution on the Kenai Peninsula as they are not indigenous to the area. They have, however, been introduced to some lakes accessible by trails, notably Grayling, Bench, Fuller, and Crescent lakes. These fish have also been successfully established in the Twin Lakes and Upper and Lower Paradise lakes, which are accessible by floatplane. Grayling are abundant at the outlets of these lakes from June through September and are most easily caught on flies and small spinners.

Dolly Varden—These sea-run char abound in most coastal streams from July through November. When these fish are in, fast action can be expected on many rivers and creeks. The Kenai River offers the best chance at lunker "dollies." They are readily taken on salmon eggs, wet flies or nymphs, and small bright lures.

Eulachon—Can be taken by long-handled dip nets during the May spawning run. Hooligan are abundant in Placer and Twentymile rivers near Portage and at the mouth of Resurrection River near Seward. There is a special subsistence gill-net fishery for these fish in the lower Kenai River during late May. Special regulations are applied to this unique fishery.

King Salmon—The king salmon season on the Anchor River, Deep

Creek, Kasilof River, and the Ninilchik River is open only for short periods of time from late May through late June. The Kenai River from the Skilak Lake outlet to its confluence with Cook Inlet is also open during a portion of the season. King salmon can be taken on a variety of spoons and spinners, but salmon egg clusters are the most popular bait. A boat is recommended for successful angling for kings in the large glacial Kenai River.

Lake Trout—Also a char, "lakers," or mackinaw, are present in all glacial lakes in the Kenai River system. Mountain lakes just prior to freezeup and shortly after breakup are recommended sites. Good catches are common during the spring and fall months by trolling the shallows with spoons or flatfish. During the winter, jigging with spoons under the ice is usually productive.

Pink Salmon—Very cyclic in most Kenai Peninsula streams, with the strong runs occurring in even-numbered years. The largest runs occur in the lower Kenai River below the Skilak Lake outlet from late July through August. Resurrection Creek near Hope is also a good stream during the same period of time.

Rainbow Trout—Found in most waters of the western Kenai Peninsula and are available throughout the year. Some rainbows run up to twenty-four inches in the upper Russian River and Russian Lakes. Salmon eggs, small lures cast from the shore or trolled, and flies are effective.

Red Salmon—Available in the Russian River from early June to late August. Colorful streamer flies used with spinning gear is a proven method for taking red salmon on the Russian River, which is a fly-fishing-only stream. This area is subject to special regulations and field emergency closures. Another location offering red salmon fishing is the English Bay area, located south of Seldovia. This is a fly-in fishery, and reds are present during the month of June. Angling for landlocked red salmon or kokanee is possible in Hidden Lake on the Skilak Loop Road.

Silver Salmon—These flashy fighters enter most peninsula streams in late July, with runs peaking during September. Silver salmon are most abundant in the Kenai River and are chiefly present from late July through October. This particular run has two peaks, which occur in early August and early September. Several lakes stock landlocked silvers. Egg clusters are preferred bait in glacial waters, while bright spoons, spinners, and streamer flies work well in clear waters.

Steelheads—This highly prized sea-run rainbow trout enters fresh water from mid-August through October, with the peak of the upstream migration occurring in September. The most popular steelhead streams are the Anchor River, Deep Creek, and the Ninilchik River. Salmon eggs, spin'n glows and okie drifters take the most fish. For the fly fisherman, fluorescent flies have proven effective on this species.

Kodiak Island

Saltwater Fishing:

Chum Salmon — Chums, or "dog" salmon, usually arrive in the area in late July and early August. Most chums are taken incidental to pink and coho salmon fishing.

Dolly Varden — Plentiful along rocky beaches from about June through July. Herring strips and small- to medium-sized lures work well.

Halibut and other marine fish — Halibut, rockfish, greenling flounder, and other marine fish are caught in this area throughout the year. However, fishing in the offshore Kodiak area is best during the summer months as fish are more active. The rockfish are taken in the shallow areas characterized by kelp and/or rock outcroppings. Any type of shiny lure will take these fish. Halibut are plentiful, but most are taken from local areas off Long and Woody islands.

Pink Salmon — The first pinks, or "humpies," move into the local beach areas in late June to early July. Fishing is usually poor until after the fourth of July. It picks up by mid-July and is good to excellent until mid-August.

Silver Salmon — Silvers are taken off Pasagshak Beach in mid-August; however, the best beach fishing is during early September.

Freshwater Fishing:

Dolly Varden — Numerous in streams all around the island. May and September are the best months. Salmon eggs, wet flies, and small lures are effective.

Grayling — These arctic fish have been successfully introduced into Cascade, Aurel, Abercrombie, and Long lakes. Shoreline fishing with dry flies is recommended.

King Salmon — The Karluk River has the only run readily accessible to Kodiak anglers and is about seventy air miles from the city. Kings start into the river during early June; however, fishing is usually poor in the upper river areas until the last week in June. About ninety percent of the kings will be in the river by July 4, and spawning will peak in mid-August.

Pink Salmon — Abundant in all streams around Kodiak and Afognak islands. July and early August are the best times to find these fish in peak condition.

Rainbow Trout — Good trout fishing during early June is available in most river-lake systems on Afognak and Kodiak islands.

Red Salmon — Found in Afognak, Uganik, Buskin and Saltery rivers in

June, and in Karluk River June 15 to September 1. Streamer flies and small lures fished very slowly work best.

Silver Salmon—Silvers enter most of the larger streams during high water in late August and early September. Good fishing is available through September in the Buskin, American, Pasagshak, Karluk, and Afognak rivers. These fish average about ten pounds and are readily taken on salmon eggs and lures.

Steelhead—The Karluk River in October is a longtime favorite with local anglers. The Frazer, Ayakulik (Red), and Saltery rivers also have runs of steelhead. Spinners with a bucktail, streamer flies, golf tees, and daredevil-type spoons are effective.

Bristol Bay

Freshwater Fishing:

Grayling—May be taken readily from May through October. They are abundant throughout the entire Bristol Bay area, but the record-breakers are found in the outlet of lower Ugashik Lake during July and August.

King Salmon—These tackle-busters are at their best from mid-June through July. The better spots are on the Naknek River near King Salmon, along the Nushagak River upstream from the village of Portage Creek, and throughout the length of the Alagnak River. Check on closures for the Naknek River.

Rainbow Trout—The connecting streams, outlets, and many tributaries of all Bristol Bay watersheds, except the Egegik and Ugashik lakes systems, offer rainbow fishing that is hard to beat. Big silvery rainbows that are often mistaken for steelhead may be taken in the Naknek and Illiamna lake drainages. The best periods are spring and fall.

Silver Salmon—Available in Bristol Bay streams from late July to mid-September. Lures such as golf tees or egg clusters work well.

Fairbanks and Northern Alaska

Freshwater Fishing:

Arctic Char and Dolly Varden—Available in coastal streams throughout the season. Most streams on the Seward Peninsula contain arctic char and dolly varden in August and September. There is also good fishing in Nenana River tributaries near Nenana, and in rivers near Kotzebue. The best fishing occurs right after breakup and in September.

Burbot — These freshwater ling cod are taken throughout the season, with fall and winter fishing the best. Good fishing is available in the Chena and Tanana rivers near Fairbanks, the Moose and Chisana rivers near Tok and George, and Harding and Fielding lakes.

Chum Salmon — Found in coastal areas July 15 to September 30, peaking in August. In interior waters they are found August 15 to November 1, peaking in September. Excellent chum salmon fisheries are found during July on the lower Nome and Niukluk rivers.

Grayling — The headwater areas of all clear-flowing rivers and streams are considered suitable grayling habitats. The best times are early and late in the season from April 1 to September 30.

King Salmon — Coastal areas from May 1 to July 30. In interior areas they are found from July 1 to August, peaking July 15.

Lake Trout — Occur throughout the season in lakes in the Brooks Range, and near Paxson. Harding Lake has a small population as a result of stocking.

Northern Pike — June 1 to September 15 is considered the best time for angling; however, large numbers enter the winter fishery also. The pike is common throughout the Interior, and trophy fish can be found in the Minto Flats area west of Fairbanks, and at East Twin and Wien lakes. Many sloughs and freshwater tributaries of the Yukon and Kuskokwim rivers contain large numbers of pike during the summer.

Pink Salmon — Available only in coastal streams June 15 to August 15, peaking in July. Excellent fishing in the Unalakleet River near Norton Sound, and in the Nome, Snake, and Niukluk rivers near Nome.

Rainbow Trout — Taken throughout the season. All populations are stocked fish except naturally occurring rainbows in the Aniak River and the Kuskokwim River drainage.

Sheefish — Taken year-round in Kotzebue Sound and the Selawick Lake area. Ice fishing on Hotham Inlet and Selawik Lake is good in late spring. During summer and fall the Kiana, Ambler, and Kobuk areas provide some of the best sheefish fishing. Limited numbers are available in the upper Chatanika River near the Steese and Elliott highways in fall, and in Fourmile Lake on the Taylor Highway. Limited numbers of sheefish may also be found in the Chena River near Fairbanks and at the mouths of clearwater tributaries of the Tanana River. Spoons (daredevils) are most commonly used to take sheefish.

Silver Salmon — In addition to occurring naturally in the river systems, silver salmon are stocked in many of the landlocked lakes.

Whitefish — These fish are plentiful in most interior and arctic Alaska streams and lakes, but they are difficult to catch. Round and humpback whitefish can be taken in streams with salmon eggs on a small hook. Excellent spearfishing is available in the entire Tanana River drainage, especially the upper Chatanika river in September and October. During the spring and summer, round whitefish may be taken near Delta Junction. Small worms and flies seem to work best.

The "Alaska Sportfishing Guide," available from the Alaska Department of Fish and Game, is designed for anglers unfamiliar with the state. This booklet contains sketch maps showing select locations of waters throughout Alaska and the type of access available. For a copy of this publication, mail $1.00 to the Alaska Department of Fish and Game, Box 3-2000, Juneau AK 99802.

Trapping

The trapping of fur-bearing animals is still widely practiced in Alaska. Animals that may be trapped include beaver, coyote, red fox, blue and white arctic fox, lynx, martin, mink, weasel (ermine), muskrat, land otter, raccoon, squirrel, marmot, wolf, and wolverine. The larger animals bring the highest price for pelts, the exact amount depending on the availability and the condition of the pelt. Traplines are worked during the winter, and seasonal work is usually needed to supplement income during the summer. A trapping license for an Alaskan resident is $10.00. For a nonresident, the license is $140.00.

Hunting

Big-game hunting in Alaska can be an unforgettable experience. Here you can hunt game that is scarce or not available at all in other states — and you can reasonably expect to bag a decent-size, perhaps even trophy-size, animal. Not only that, the hunting trip alone can be an experience. Many people hunting in Alaska secure the services of a registered big-game hunting guide, and such guides subscribe to the policy of fair chase. While they will often use aircraft to fly hunters and their gear into the backcountry, the actual hunting is done on foot from base camps. Some guides offer horseback hunts with horses and pack animals. Others use boats on rivers and lakes in the backcountry to get to areas not otherwise accessible. In coastal areas some guide services use large boats as the base camp itself, and small rafts and canoes for mobility in shallower areas. Along the coast there is the added advantage of an abundance of fresh seafood. In any case, hunting and fishing trips can always be combined to provide fresh food, even in inland areas where there is usually at least a stream close by to provide the fish.

There are twenty-six game management areas in Alaska, and seasons, bag limits, rules, and regulations in each area may change slightly from year to year. A copy of "Alaska Hunting Regulations" for the year in which you wish to hunt should be obtained from the Alaska Department of Fish and Game, Box 3-2000, Juneau AK 99802.

For most big game, there is usually either a season in the fall and one in the spring, or else the season runs from early fall to late spring. Licenses can be obtained by mail from the Licensing Section, Alaska Department of Revenue, 1107 West Eighth Street, Juneau AK 99801. No hunting licenses are issued at Alaska Fish and Game offices.

All nonresidents are required by Alaska law to have a guide when hunting brown and grizzly bear or Dall sheep. This must be either a registered guide or a relative over nineteen years of age within the second degree of kindred. (The second degree of kindred includes only parents, children, sisters and brothers, grandparents, and grandchildren.) Also, any *resident or nonresident* person sixteen years of age or older hunting waterfowl must have on his person a signed federal migratory bird hunting stamp (duck stamp).

License fees for residents of Alaska are as follows:

Hunting:	$ 12.00
Hunting and sportfishing:	$ 22.00
Hunting and trapping:	$ 22.00
Trapping:	$ 10.00

For nonresidents the license fees are as follows:

Hunting:	$ 60.00
Hunting and sportfishing:	$ 96.00
Hunting and trapping:	$200.00
Trapping:	$140.00

In addition to purchasing a valid hunting license, nonresidents hunting big-game animals must purchase a metal locking tag that must be affixed to the animal immediately upon capture, and that must remain there until the animal is prepared for storage, consumed, or exported. Locking tags are required of residents only for brown/grizzly bear and musk-oxen. All tag fees are as follows:

Resident tag fees:

Brown/grizzly bear:	$ 25.00
Musk-oxen, bull:	$500.00
Musk-oxen, cow:	$ 25.00

Nonresident tag fees:

Black bear:	$200.00
Brown/grizzly bear:	$350.00
Bison:	$350.00

Caribou:	$ 300.00
Deer:	$ 135.00
Elk:	$ 250.00
Goat:	$ 250.00
Moose:	$ 300.00
Musk-oxen:	$1,100.00
Sheep:	$ 400.00
Wolf:	$ 150.00
Wolverine:	$ 150.00

A listing of master guides and the game management units in which they are licensed to guide follows. For a listing of registered guides (in addition to the master guides listed here) write: State of Alaska, Department of Commerce and Economic Development, Division of Occupational Licensing, Pouch D, Juneau AK 99511.

Following the listing of master guides is a list of wilderness lodges and resorts all over the state of Alaska. Most of these lodges are not accessible by highway, and most specialize in sportfishing and sport-hunting vacation packages, which often include other activities as well, such as rafting, hiking, backpacking, campouts, photography, and flightseeing. Most offer brochures and price lists detailing all activities offered, length of stay, equipment and gear provided, and the transportation arrangements necessary to get to and from the lodge. (Often transportation is included as part of the package price.)

Master Guides

Information in columns as follows: Lefthand column, name and address; middle, license number; righthand, game management areas. Areas 1–26 are designated on map, p. 170; area 27 is offshore and not currently open to hunting.

Anchorage:

Dennis I. Branham P.O. Box 6184 Annex Anchorage AK 99502	AA 002	1–27
Clark L. Engle 4129 Lana Court Anchorage AK 99504	AA 029	1–27
Kirk Gay Box 6583 Anchorage AK 99502	AA 045	9, 17, 19

Ward I. Gay 6240 E. 112th Anchorage AK 99503	AA 018	1–27
James Harrower SRA Box 809 Anchorage AK 99502	AA 049	6–27
Joe Hendricks P.O. Box 2104 Anchorage AK 99510	AA 032	6–17, 22, 23, 26, 27
Keith N. Johnson 3646 North Point Drive Anchorage AK 99502	AA 035	6–9, 11–17, 20
John J. Lee P.O. Box 4-2495 Anchorage AK 99509	AA 025	6–17, 19, 22, 23, 26, 27
John S. Swiss 129 F. Street Anchorage AK 99501	AA 031	6–27
Ben C. White 513 F Street Anchorage AK 99501	AA 044	1–27

Bethel:

Keith C. Koontz P.O. Box 2027 Bethel AK 99559	AA 046	18–27

Chugiak:

Harvey D. Harms Box 71 Chugiak AK 99567	AA 048	6–27

Cold Bay:

Donald L. Johnson P.O. Box 102 Cold Bay AK 99571	AA 033	6–27

Fairbanks:

Lynn M. Castle c/o Box 1616 Fairbanks AK 99707	AA 039	18–27

Bernd Gaedeke P.O. Box 80424 Fairbanks AK 99708	AA 043	18–27
Charles Lee Gray 311 Slater Street Fairbanks AK 99701	AA 028	6–27
Harmon R. Helmericks Via 930 Ninth Avenue Fairbanks AK 99701	AA 004	18–27

Gakona:

C.M. "Bud" Conkle Star Route Box 350 Gakona AK 99586	AA 019	6–27
BIll Ellis Star Route Box 370 Gakona AK 99586	AA 034	6–27
Leland R. Hancock Nabesna Road Gakona AK 99586	AA 026	6–17
Cleo B. McMahan Box 7 Gakona AK 99586	AA 050	1–27

Homer:

John H. McLay Box 754 Homer AK 99603	AA 015	6–21, 24, 25, 27
Jess Willard Box 375 Caribou Lake Homer AK 99603	AA 022	6–27

Hoonah:

Frank See, Sr. P.O. Box 136 Hoonah AK 99829	AA 005	1–5

Hope:

| Keith W. Specking
P.O. Box 18
Hope AK 99605 | AA 023 | 6–17 |

Juneau:

| Marcus F. Jensen
P.O. Box 2220
Juneau AK 99803 | AA 020 | 1–5, 18–21, 24, 25, 27 |

| Karl E. Lane
P.O. Box 295
Juneau AK 99802 | AA 010 | 1–7, 11–16 |

Kasilof:

| George R. Pollard
P.O. Box 40
Kasilof AK 99610 | AA 014 | 6–17 |

Kodiak:

| Leon Francisco
P.O. Box 483
Kodiak AK 99615 | AA 041 | 6–17 |

Kotzebue:

| Nelson Walker
P.O. Box 57
Kotzebue AK 99752 | AA 003 | 18–27 |

North Pole:

| Leroy Shebal
Box 55441
North Pole AK 99705 | AA 017 | 6–27 |

Palmer:

| George E. Palmer
Box 878
Palmer AK 99645 | AA 047 | 6, 16, 19 |

Andy R. Runyan Star Route C, Box 8860 Palmer AK 99645	AA 040	1–27

Port Alsworth:

Jay S. Hammond General Delivery Port Alsworth AK 99653	AA 009	6–27

Sitka:

Tarleton F. Smith P.O. Box 1132 Sitka AK 99835	AA 030	1–5

Sterling:

Ray McNutt Box 10 Sterling AK 99672	AA 038	6–27

Tok:

John E. Erickson Box 101 Tok AK 99780	AA 037	1–7, 11–16, 18–21, 24, 25, 27

Wasilla:

Bob Buzby Box 344 Wasilla AK 99687	AA 013	6–27
Douglas B. Vaden General Delivery Wasilla AK 99687	AA 036	12, 18, 19, 27

Wiseman:

Richard E. Reakoff General Delivery Wiseman AK 99726	AA 042	18–27

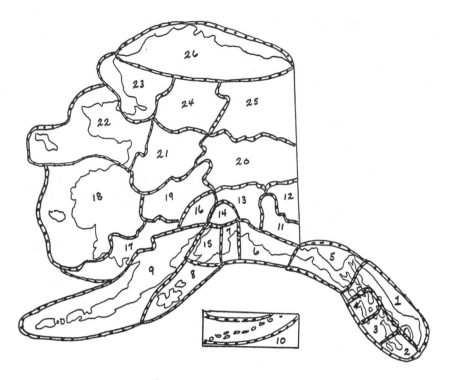

Game management areas.

Wilderness Lodges and Resorts

Southeast:

Bell Island Hot Springs
1113 5th Ave. So., #108
Edmonds WA 98020

Sportfishing lodge north of Ketchi-kan. Cabins, restaurant, cocktails, swimming. Specializes in king and silver salmon.

Elfin Cove Sportfishing Chalet
Dennis Hay
Glacier View
Elfin Cove AK 99825

Exclusive accommodations for eight guests eighty-six miles west of Juneau on Chichagof Island. Three-, four-, and six-day fishing packages include meals, boats, guide, and tackle.

Fireweed Lodge
Box 116
Klawock AK 99925

Stream, lake, and saltwater fishing. Lodge ½ mile east of Klawock on Klawock River. Bicycles, canoes, boats, and gear available.

George Inlet Lodge
Hank Van Lear
Box 5077
Ketchikan AK 99901

Fresh and saltwater fishing lodge on the edge of Misty Fjords National Monument. Family-style meals and wet bar. Accommodations for twenty-five. Boat and plane charters available.

Glacier Bay Lodge
Box 108
Gustavus AK 99826

Lodge at Bartlett Cove in Glacier Bay National Park and Preserve, sixty-six air miles west of Juneau. Fifty-five rooms, all facilities.

Gustavus Inn
JoAnn Lesh
Box 31
Gustavus AK 99826

Located in Gustavus nine miles from Glacier Bay Park headquarters. Twenty rooms, family-style meals in homestead atmosphere. Boat and air tours, charter fishing, bicycling.

Karta Inn
Box 114
Craig AK 99921

Remote waterfront lodge on Prince of Wales Island. Fishing and sightseeing tours from twenty-four-foot cruiser. Fish smoking and canning.

Kootznahoo Inlet Lodge
Albert Kookesh
Box 134
Angoon AK 99820

Ten-unit motel on Admiralty Island. Kitchens in six units in addition to full-service dining room. Charter boat fishing and skiff and motor rentals.

Log Cabin Sports Rental, Inc.
Skip Fabry
Box 54
Klawock AK 99925

Rustic cabins on the beach. Two restaurants within walking distance. Sportfishing packages, salmon charters, canoe trips, and mountain lake fly-ins.

Misty Fjords Resort
Michael B. Salazar
Ketchikan Air Service
Box 6900
Ketchikan AK 99901

Sixty-two miles south of Ketchikan on five-mile-long glacier-carved lake. Groups of two to six for do-it-yourself trout fishing. Daily or weekly rates available on request.

Prince of Wales Lodge
Ralph Burnett
Box 72
Klawock AK 99925

In Klawock on Prince of Wales Island. Twelve rooms with bath and shower on waterfront. Fresh- and saltwater sportfishing for salmon, trout, halibut, steelhead. Sport hunting in season.

Salmon River Rentals
Rita and Eldon Wilson
Box 121
Gustavus AK 99826

Housekeeping cabins located in wooded area of Glacier Bay National Park. Sportfishing, hiking, kayaking, and cycling. Free pickup and delivery to and from airport.

Taku Glacier Lodge
195 South Franklin Street
Juneau AK 99801

Located thirty air miles from Juneau on the Taku River, this log lodge was built in 1923 at the base of 3500-foot mountains with five advancing glaciers within five miles. Daily salmon bake.

Thayer Lake Lodge
Bob Nelson
Box 5416
Ketchikan AK 99901

Wilderness lodge on Admiralty Island, sixty miles southwest of Juneau. Trout fishing, boating and hiking. Lodge accommodates twelve, and room for eight more is provided by two cabins.

Thunderbird Lodge
Frank See
Box 136
Hoonah AK 99829

Rustic log cabin lodge near the Tlingit village of Hoonah on scenic Neka Bay. Small groups in family-style environment. Fresh- and saltwater sportfishing.

Unuk River Post
Henry Aegerter
Box 5065
Ketchikan AK 99901

Individual log cabins located sixty-five miles northeast of Ketchikan on the Alaska mainland. Riverboats, canoes, and guides for trout and salmon fishing.

Waterfall Resort
Box 6440
Ketchikan AK 99901

Wilderness resort at site of former cannery sixty-two miles northwest of Ketchikan. Clam beaches and sportfishing. Cabin or hotel accommodations.

Yes Bay Lodge
The Hack Family
Yes Bay AK 99950

Sportfishing lodge located fifty miles northwest of Ketchikan on secluded inlet. Fish smoking services available. Family dining features fresh Alaska seafood. All facilities.

Southcentral:

Adventures Unlimited
Jim and Vonnie Grimes
Box 89
Cantwell AK 99729

Year-round lodge located at mile 100 of the Denali Highway (8) thirty-five miles east of Cantwell. Caters to winter tours, snowmobiling, and skiing. Full facilities, self-contained.

Alaska Safari, Inc.
Box 6583
Anchorage AK 99502

Exclusive sportfishing lodge. Specializes in stream fishing for eight species of trophy fish. Accommodations for sixteen persons.

Alaska Wilderness Safaris, Inc.
Box 8512
Star Route C
Palmer AK 99645

Complete visitor facility located between the Talkeetna and Chugach mountains. Hiking, horseback riding, and backpacking trips. Transportation from Anchorage furnished.

Alexander Lake Lodge
Ken Clark
Box 4-212
Anchorage AK 99509

Lodge located on Alexander Lake fifty air miles northwest of Anchorage. Family dining and bar. Big-game hunting, sportfishing, and birdwatching. Area home of trumpeter swan.

Bear Track Lodge
Jere F. Griffin
Box 3-385
Anchorage AK 99501

Remote lodge twenty-five miles west of Cordova. Accommodations for twelve people are provided by individual cabins. Charter yacht for glacier tours on Prince William Sound.

Betz Guide Service
Richard and Lavelle Betz
Box 4-2053
Anchorage AK 99509

Large main lodge located about seventy air miles northwest of Anchorage in McKinley foothills with remote spike camps. Small groups for sportfishing, sport hunting and flightseeing.

Branham Adventures
Dennis Branham
Box 6184
Anchorage AK 99502

Sportfishing and hunting lodge on Finger Lake ninety-nine miles northwest of Anchorage on the south side of the Alaska range. Exclusive use of aircraft with personal guide and pilot.

Call of the Wild
Star Route A
Box 2594
Big Lake AK 99687

Two cabins, restaurant, and bar located at the west end of Big Lake north of Anchorage. Sportfishing, waterskiing, boating, hiking, and ice fishing. Accessible by four-wheel-drive vehicle.

Chulitna River Lodge
Mr. and Mrs. Stephen Hanson
Star Route B, Box 374A
Willow AK 99688

Comfortable log cabins on lake at mile 156 of the Parks Highway in Denali State Park. Canyon rafting, hiking, fishing for salmon, trout, grayling, and dolly varden. Licenses available.

Evergreen Lodge
Alaska River Guides
Paul and Cheryl Holland
Star Route C, Box 8867
Palmer AK 99645

Main lodge, cabins, and bunkhouse overlooking Lake Louise. Guided fishing float trips for trout, salmon, and grayling. Cross-country skiing in winter. Full facilities include sauna, tackle shop, grocery, and package store.

Gray Bow Lodge
David and Mary Kay McDivitt
Box 4-3034
Anchorage AK 99509

Lodge on the Talachulitna River is rustic but comfortable. All meals, bar. Maximum of four people per week. Rainbow and grayling available all summer, salmon in season.

Gwin's Lodge
Mile 52 Sterling Highway
Cooper Landing AK 99572

Five motel units and camper spaces located at mile 52 Sterling Highway on the Kenai Peninsula. Nearby trails, lakes, streams. Charter fishing in Cook Inlet and Kenai River.

Hideaway
Star Route C, Box 8860
Palmer AK 99645

Lodge on Lake Louise seventeen miles from Mile 160 of the Glenn Highway. Accessible by boat or plane only.

Katchemak Bay Wilderness
  Lodge
Diane McBride
China Poot Bay
Homer AK 99603

Year-round lodge on the Kenai Peninsula across the bay from Homer. Hikes, shrimping, crabbing, guided sportfishing, and duck hunting. Wildlife photography. Private cabins.

King Bear Lodge
Andrew J. Piekarski
P.O. Box 831
Eagle River AK 99577

Rustic wilderness camp at confluence of Lake Creek and the Yentna River sixty-seven miles northwest of Anchorage. Fishing for salmon, trout, pike and grayling. Five cabins, sauna, family-style meals.

Lake Creek Lodge
Dean E. Salmeir,
  SKS Outfitter
Box 8-229
Anchorage AK 99508

Wilderness lodge sixty-five miles northwest of Anchorage at confluence of Lake Creek and the Yentna River. Sportfishing and hunting for moose and black bear.

Lake Louise Lodge
Star Route C, Box 8870
Palmer AK 99645

Sportfishing lodge on Lake Louise with cabins and camping facilities. Restaurant and bar. Swimming, waterskiing, and ice fishing.

McCarthy Lodge
Bernd Hoffman
General Delivery
Glennallen AK 99588

Lodge located in historic town in the Wrangell Mountains near the old Kennicott copper mine. Tours of old mine, cabins, and buildings dating from 1900. Tour transportation available.

Martana Lodge, SKS Outfitters
Box 8-829
Anchorage AK 99508

Remote hunting and fishing lodge ninety-nine miles northwest of Anchorage. Guided hunts for moose and black bear. Ten-guest maximum.

Montana Creek Lodge
Star Route A, Box 560
Willow AK 99688

Sportfishing lodge with cabins and camper sites located at mile 96.5 George Parks Highway. Bar and restaurant with live entertainment weekends.

Mystic Lake Lodge
George Palmer, Master Guide
Box 878
Palmer AK 99645

Rustic lodge for eight to ten people located 160 air miles northwest of Anchorage. Sportfishing, photography, water sports, mountain climbing. Family meals. Open year-round. Air access only.

Northwest Outfitters, Inc.
Chris Goll
8311 Arctic Blvd.
Anchorage AK 99502

Located on the Kenai Peninsula on the banks of the Kenai River five miles below Skilak Lake. Main lodge and individual cabins. Family-style meals. Accessible by road and floatplane.

Prince William Sound Inn
M.J. Adkins
Port Oceanic
Knight Island
via Cordova AK 99574

Rustic sportfishing and hunting lodge located on Knight Island in Prince William Sound about ninety-three miles southeast of Anchorage. Home-cooked family-style meals. Marine fuel is available.

Rainy Pass Lodge
C. Vernon Humble
3900 Amber Bay Loop
Anchorage AK 99502

Main lodge located 124 miles northwest of Anchorage on Puntilla Lake is accessible only by air. Side camps are cabins and high-wall tents with wooden floor. Electricity, running water, and oil heat.

Sadie Cove Wilderness Lodge
Keith Iverson
Box 2265
Homer AK 99603

Sportfishing lodge on the Kenai Peninsula accessible by floatplane out of Homer. Three cabins and dining room. Bath house with sauna on beach. Outside plumbing.

Sheep Mountain Lodge
Star Route C, Box 8490
Palmer AK 99645

Cabins, trailer, and camper sites located at mile 113.5 Glenn Highway, sixty-five miles northeast of Palmer. Hot tub, sauna, and washateria.

Silvertip Lodges
Box 6389
Anchorage AK 99502

Two wilderness fly-in lodges at the headwaters and mouth of the Talachulitna River, seventy-five miles northwest of Anchorage. Rates include meals, guide service, equipment, and boats.

Stephan Lake Adventures
Box 307
Talkeetna AK 99676

Fly-in lodge and cabins for sport-fishing, hiking, and photography. Lodge located on Stephan Lake in the Talkeetna Mountains.

Stephan Lake Lodge
Jim Baily
Box 695
Eagle River AK 99577

Comfortable rustic accommodations at this remote lodge in the Talkeetna Mountains. Main lodge and seven cabins, family meals, wet bar. Guided big-game hunting and sportfishing.

Talachulitna River Lodge
Robert C. Gastrock, Tal., Inc.
Box 6595
Anchorage AK 99502

Full-service lodge at the mouth of the river seventy-five miles northwest of Anchorage. Seven private rooms. Sportfishing package includes everything but transportation from Anchorage.

Talahiem Lodge
Mark E. Miller, Outfitter
General Delivery
Skwentna AK 99667

Wilderness lodge for guided sportfishing and hunting tours. Radio phone 345-1160 KEL-43.

Tal-A-View Lodge
Alaska Outdoors Travel Svc.
Box 6324
Anchorage AK 99502

Sportfishing lodge located sixty-five miles west of Anchorage, 300 feet from the Tal River. Access by both plane and floatplane. Fish include five species of salmon, rainbow, and dolly varden.

A Wilderness Place
Mike Keim
Skwentna AK 99667

Sportfishing lodge on Lake Creek, sixty-five miles northwest of Anchorage. Log cabins accommodate six. Guided fishing, riverboat service, and float trips.

Willard's Moose Camp
George Willard
Master Guide and Outfitter
Caribou Lake
Homer AK 99603

Sportfishing and hunting at Caribou Lake on the Kenai Peninsula. Camp meals, lodging, boats and horses. Sport hunting and photography is by contract only.

Willow Lake Lodge
Hank Nosek
Box 149
Willow AK 99688

Lakeside lodge with view of Mount McKinley is located at mile 69.5 George Parks Highway. All facilities. Fishing, hunting, gold panning, rafting, berrying, and dogsled rides.

Yentna Station Roadhouse
Dan Gabryszak
Alaska River Touring Co.
Box 1884
Anchorage AK 99510

Located eighty-five miles northwest of Anchorage on the Yentna River, this year-round fishing and hunting lodge is on the historic Iditarod Trail. Fishing for salmon, trout, grayling, and pike. Hunting for moose and black bear.

Interior and Far North:

Alatna Lodge
Box 80424
Fairbanks AK 99708

Outfitting point for Alatna Guide Service. Lodge located north of the treeline in arctic tundra features floats, hiking, fishing, and hunting.

Arctic Circle Hot Springs
Roger and Dianne Merrill
Central AK 99730

Hot springs resort hotel built in 1930s has all modern amenities, including Jacuzzi on each floor, indoor swimming pool, and saloon.

Arctic Tern Lodge
James Shoffner
Box 425
Nenana AK 99760

Sportfishing lodge and individual cabins located on Wien Lake 99 air miles southwest of Fairbanks. Plane available for guest use. Flightseeing tours of Denali National Park.

Black Spruce Lodge
Leston McNeil
Box 333
Delta Junction AK 99737

Located on Quartz Lake just off the Richardson Highway, this sportfishing lodge ferries guests to and from camp by riverboat. Boats and motors included. Swimming and waterskiing.

Brooks Range Arctic Hunt
Mile 329 Parks Hwy, Route 1
Nenana AK 99760

Guided hunting, fishing, and canoeing available at the nine-unit lodge on the George Parks Highway. Food and cooking equipment provided.

Camp Bendeleben
John W. Elmore, Outfitter
Box 1045
Nome AK 99762

An early–1900s gold mining camp located about seventy-five miles northeast of Nome in Council. Two private cabins sleep four with meals in lodge. Open year-round for fishing and small game hunting.

Camp Denali
Wally Cole
Box 67
Denali National Park AK
    99755

Wilderness vacation retreat located within Denali National Park. Features bush country living, hiking, gold panning, photo workshop, guide program. All expense vacation or cabins.

Chatanika Gold Camp
S.R. 20671
Fairbanks AK 99701

Twelve-unit lodge located at mile 27 Steese Highway features fishing, hunting, hiking, canoeing, and wildlife photography. Open year-round.

Chena Hot Springs Resort
Roger Cotting
1919 Lathrop Street
Fairbanks AK 99701

This year-round resort features an indoor hot springs pool, a restaurant and bar, and choice of room, suite, or cabin. Cross-country skiing, hiking, climbing, games, picnics. Located sixty miles northeast of Fairbanks on Chena Hot Springs Road.

Colville Village
930 9th Avenue
Fairbanks AK 99701

Year-round lodge with three rental units that include showers, food, and full bedding facilities. Features guides, wildlife, boating, and hunting.

Copper Lake Fish Camp
Mrs. R. Frederick
Mile 28 Nabesna Road
Gakona AK 99586

Lodge on the shore of Copper Lake in the scenic Wrangell Mountain wilderness. Main lodge and four cabins provide accommodations. Boats and motors are available.

Denali Wilderness Lodges
Wood River Lodge
Lynn Castle
Box 517
Denali National Park AK
    99755

The Wood River Lodge is located forty miles east of Denali National Park and offers an authentic wilderness experience. One-, two-, and five-day tour packages are available. Dogsled excursions are featured in winter.

The Caches
Al Wright
Box 60531
Fairbanks AK 99706

Sportfishing camp thirty-four miles northwest of Fairbanks. Camp has cabins, boats, fishing gear, and gas cooking facilities. Flights to camp are provided. Species include pike, sheefish, and whitefish.

Farewell Lake Lodge
Stan Frost
McGrath AK 99627

Wilderness lodge accepts only eight guests at a time to preserve atmosphere. Located 139 miles northwest of Anchorage. Float and jet boat trips, sailboats, canoes. Private airstrip with aircraft available.

Iniakuk Lake Lodge
Bernd Gaedeke
Box 80424
Fairbanks AK 99708

Wilderness lodge located above the Arctic Circle in the Brooks Range. Sportfishing, float trips, scenic flights, guided hunts. Spring skiing, snowmobiling, and ice fishing. Bilingual English and German.

Jack River Inn
Box 8
Cantwell AK 99729

Located at mile 210 George Parks Highway, lodge is open year-round. Features ten rental units with showers, food, and full bedding facilities.

Kroto Lake Retreat
Sepp Weber
Box 10-1663
Anchorage AK 99511

Rustic retreat located south of Denali National Park is accessible over a two-mile trail from the Petersville Road. Baggage transport is provided. Ski lodge with maintained trails in winter.

Manley Lodge
Manley Hot Springs AK
 99756

This lodge features hunting, fishing, boating, and photography. Seven units at mile 163 Elliott Highway.

Melozi Hot Springs Lodge
Box 80562
Fairbanks AK 99708

Lodge features natural hot springs, indoor pool, wet bar and family meals. Located 200 air miles northwest of Fairbanks. Fishing and big-game photography.

Midnight Sun Lodge
Phil Driver, Registered Guide
1306 E. 26th Avenue
Anchorage AK 99504

Wilderness lodge on the northwest Arctic coast ninety miles northwest of Kotzebue. Main lodge and cabins with modern facilities. Features backpack-float trips, photo-safaris, and guided hunting.

Midway Lodge
Star Route Box 90684
Fairbanks AK 99701

Sportfishing and big-game hunting lodge located at mile 49 Richardson Highway. Ice fishing in winter. Accommodations for sixteen with restaurant and lounge.

One-O-One Lodge
S.R. 20035
Fairbanks AK 99701

Summer lodge located at mile 101 Steese Highway. There are four units available. Hiking and wildlife viewing are featured activities.

Ruby Roadhouse
Jim Hart
Box 6
Ruby AK 99768

Comfortable historic country inn located in the gold rush town of Ruby on the Yukon River. Fishing, floating, canoeing by day or week. Private plane for sightseeing. Accessible by commercial flights from Fairbanks or Galena.

Salchaket Homestead
S.R. 90646
Fairbanks AK 99701

Year-round lodge forty miles south of Fairbanks at mile 322 Richardson Highway. Ten units with showers, food, and cocktail lounge. Fish, boat, and hike trips.

Silvertip on the Unalakleet
Box 6389
Anchorage AK 99502

Limited bookings at this private fishing lodge located on the Unalakleet River, eight miles from a native village. Trophy-size char, salmon, and grayling.

Sportsmen's Paradise Lodge
Mrs. R. Frederick
Gakona AK 99586

Located near Twin Lakes at mile 28 Nabesna Road, this sportfishing lodge has a gas pump, bar, and sandwiches. Good photography in area.

Tanada Lake Lodge
Vincent P. Guzzardi
Box 258
Fairbanks AK 99707

Sportfishing and wildlife lodge high in the Wrangell Mountains on five-mile-long lake. Rustic but modern lodge and cabins with family dining. Boats, motors, and fuel provided. Open June through September.

Walker Lake Lodge
Harmon Helmericks,
  Master Guide
930 Ninth Avenue
Fairbanks AK 99701

Wilderness lodge features trips to Gates of the Arctic National Park. Also raft trips, sailing, fishing, hunting, and exploring. Accommodations in cabins; boats available.

Wilderness Fishing & Hunting
Bob Elliot
5920 Airport Way
Fairbanks AK 99701

Pilot/guide/outfitter has cabins and tent camps at fourteen different lake and river locations in interior Alaska. Boats with motors, raft trips by floatplane, guided hunting and hiking.

Wilderness Wildlife Camps
Mile 329 Parks Highway, Rt. 1
Nenana AK 99760

Fishing, hiking, canoeing, and wildlife-viewing from sixteen spike camps with walled tents. Camps are located in the Brooks Range. Meals provided.

Wiseman Lodge
Dan L. Wetzel
P.O. Box 10224
Fairbanks AK 99701

Historic lodge in central Brooks Range near the haul road and Gates of the Arctic. Features horse-drawn covered wagon rides to 1800s gold camps. Also trail rides, camping trips, backpacking tours, and Koyukuk float trips. Family-style meals.

Western and Southwest:

Afognak Wilderness Lodge
Roy Randall
Seal Bay AK 99697

Lodge located on Afognak Island between Homer and Kodiak. Year-round lodge accommodates twelve guests for salt- and freshwater fishing and photo safaris. High concentration of land and sea mammals and birds. Family-style meals.

Alaska River Safaris
Ron Hyde
4909 Rollins Drive
Anchorage AK 99504

Guided fishing at two deluxe heated tent camps located in Togiak National Wildlife Refuge—one river camp, one fly-in camp. Float trips to remote sportfishing location. Accommodations for twelve.

Alaska Trophy Lodge
R.L. Woodward
Box 4-1951
Anchorage AK 99509

Modern lodge overlooking Lake Aleknagik in the Wood River-Tikchik Lakes region, twenty miles north of Dillingham. Package includes lodging, meals, use of aircraft and boats with guides.

Alaska West River Tours
John B. Garry
P.O. Box 24
Aleknagik AK 99555

This tour company rents completely equipped wilderness fly-in camps that include shelters, boats, motors, gas, and cooking utensils. Camps are located in Wood River–Tikchik Lakes area.

Alaska's Lake Clark Lodge
Reservations Office
7320 Sixth Avenue
Tacoma WA 98406

Full facility lodge on shores of Lake Clark, 180 miles southwest of Anchorage. Offers family plan for guided fly-in trophy fishing and float trips. Brochures available on request.

Aniak Lodge
Lou Brooks
P.O. Box 83
Aniak AK 99557

One block from the Kuskokwim River in Aniak, this old lodge has fourteen units, homestyle meals and soup-and-sandwich lunches. Open year-round.

Battle Lake Lodge
Wien Air Alaska
4100 International Airport Rd.
Anchorage AK 99502

Rustic wilderness lodge located on Battle Lake in Bristol Bay trophy fish area. Accessible only by air.

Battle River Wilderness Camp
Ben C. White, Master Guide
1513 F Street
Anchorage AK 99501

Sportfishing and big-game hunting lodge on Alaska Peninsula south-west of Anchorage. Trophy fishing and guided hunts for brown and grizzly bear, bull moose, and caribou. Cabins and meals.

Bear Lake Lodge
Don Johnson
Box 152
Kenai AK 99611

Located on the western Alaska coast at Bear Lake with views of mountains and wildlife. Lounge and family-style dining, rooms in lodge or individual cabins for six to ten persons.

Becharof Lodge
Lorrie Bartlett
Box 104
Egegik AK 99579

Lodge serves Katmai National Monument and Becharof Wildlife Refuge. On the Egegik River forty-five miles from King Salmon, this wilderness fishing lodge handles large groups. Rates include guides and planes.

Becharof Lodge and Camps
Ben Guild
Box 632
Eagle River AK 99577

Located at head of Egegik River and Becharof Lake fifty miles southwest of King Salmon, lodge features sportfishing, unguided hunts, and wildlife photographic safaris.

Bristol Bay Lodge
Maggie Garry and Ron
  McMillan
Box 6349
Anchorage AK 99502

Sportfishing lodge located 300 miles southwest of Anchorage in Wood-Tikchik region. Week-long package includes room, board, daily fly-out, and transportation to and from lodge from Dillingham.

Brooks Lodge
Wien Air Alaska, Tour Dept.
4797 Business Pk. Blvd.,
  Suite G
Anchorage AK 99503

Fly-in lodge operated by Wien Air Alaska in Katmai National Monument at mouth of Brooks River. Daily tours to Valley of 10,000 Smokes. Air service to lodge from King Salmon.

Copper River Fly Fishing
  Lodge
Bob Walker
Box 260, Star Rt. 1
Kenai AK 99611

Lodge near Lake Iliamna offers room and board in comfortable tent houses. Fly fishing for rainbows and sockeye salmon. After June 15 write Pope Vanoy Landing, Iliamna, Alaska 99606.

Eberhard's Guide Service
Suzi Brunner
Box 6868
Anchorage AK 99502

The Iliamna River Lodge on the Iliamna River offers family meals, backpacking, float trips and photo safaris. Prime bear-viewing area and excellent sportfishing. Transportation from Iliamna is provided.

Ekwok Lodge
Jeff McIver
Ekwok AK 99580

Sportfishing lodge located sixty miles northeast of Dillingham on the Nushagak River. Amenities include steambath and sauna. Meals are included.

Enchanted Lake Lodge
Ed Seller
Box 97
King Salmon AK 99613

Lodge located on Alaska Peninsula sixty-two miles east of King Salmon near Kulik Lake. The lodge has sportfishing accommodations for four. Open June 1 through October 10.

Fishing Unlimited
Ken Owsichek
Box 301
Anchorage AK 99502

Daily fly-out sportfishing from main lodge and cabins. All modern amenities including sauna. Serving Iliamna, Lake Clark, and Tikchik Lakes regions. Trophy sport hunting in season.

Golden Horn Lodge
Bud Hodson
Box 6748
Anchorage AK 99502

Sportfishing lodge located in Wood-Tikchik area offers daily fly-outs, outcamps, and overnight trips to remote locations. Fishing for twelve species of sportfish.

Grosvenor Lake Lodge
Angler's Paradise Sportfishing
Wien Air Alaska
4797 Business Pk. Blvd.,
    Suite G
Anchorage AK 99503

Lodge in Katmai National Monument between Lake Coville and Lake Grosvenor is operated by Wien Air Alaska. Accommodations for eight with meals, lodging, guides, boats, and motors. Lodge is accessible by air from King Salmon.

Igiugig Lodge
Elizabeth Todd
P.O. Box 1395
Wasilla AK 99687

Wilderness lodge located on west end of Lake Iliamna, 250 air miles from Anchorage. Main lodge and cabins provide accommodations for eight. Meals, guides, and boats are included.

Iliamna Lake Lodge
Gregory Galik
921 W. 6th Ave., Suite 200
Anchorage AK 99501

Sportfishing lodge only four miles from Iliamna Airport. Also offers fly fishing seminars, raft trips and photographic safaris. Open year-round.

Iliaska Lodge
Box 28
Iliamna AK 99606

Lodge on Lake Iliamna caters only to fly fishermen. Fly-out trips for arctic char, rainbow trout, grayling, and salmon.

Kohanok Lodge
Michael Branham
Box 6128 Annex
Anchorage AK 99502

Fly-out fishing lodge on east bay of Lake Iliamna. Sportfishing package includes all planes, boats, guides, and meals. Accommodations for up to eight people.

Koksetna Camp
Chuck and Sara Hornberger
Box 69
Iliamna AK 99606

Comfortable accommodations, hot showers, and family-style meals at this wilderness lodge on Lake Clark. Photography workshop, float trips, backpacking, and sportfishing by boat.

Kulik Lodge
Anglers Paradise Sportfishing
Wien Air Alaska
4797 Business Pk. Blvd.,
    Suite G
Anchorage AK 99503

Lodge is located in Bristol Bay region near Kulik and Nonvianuk lakes. Accommodations include main lodge with fireplace and game room, and log cabins. Rates include guides, boats, and meals. Accessible only by air.

Kvichak Lodge
Edward M. Clark
Box 37
Naknek AK 99633

Guided sportfishing lodge on the Kvichak River near Lake Iliamna. Trophy fishing for rainbows, grayling, arctic char, lake trout, and sockeye salmon. Price includes guides, boats, and motors.

Lakeside Lodge
Bill Johnson
Lake Clark
Port Alsworth AK 99653

Completely modern sporting lodge for eight guests bordering Lake Clark National Park. Guided trips for trophy fishing, backpacking, and photography as well as trophy hunting August through December.

Munsey's Bear Camp
Park Munsey
Amook Pass AK 99615

Lodge located on Kodiak Island, seventy miles southwest of Kodiak. Small groups of five to six people for camera safaris and sportfishing.

Newhalen Lodge
Bill Sims
Box 2521
Anchorage AK 99510

Sportfishing lodge near Lake Iliamna. Daily fly-outs to stream fishing locations. Excellent accommodations and personalized service.

Nonvianuk Camp
Wien Air Alaska
4797 Business Pk. Blvd.,
  Suite G
Anchorage AK 99503

Rustic camp located on Nonvianuk Lake in Bristol Bay region at Branch River. Float trips on Branch system begin from camp. Area is known for its trophy-size fish.

No-See-Um Lodge
John Holman
Box 934
Palmer AK 99645

Named for the tiny hard-to-see but persistent gnats called "no-see-ums," this fly-in wilderness lodge caters to trophy sportfishermen in groups of seven per week. Thirty-five miles south of Lake Iliamna.

Patterson's Lodge
Dana Patterson
Box 43
Iliamna AK 99606

Float-equipped aircraft provide fly-out trips to wilderness for photography and fishing. Located in Bristol Bay area, the lodge serves family meals and provides picnic lunches. Winter address: Box 6366, Anchorage AK 99502.

Prestage's Sportfishing Lodge
John Prestage
Box 213
King Salmon AK 99613

Lodging, guide services, and tackle furnished for both spin and fly casting. Located on the Naknek River near King Salmon. Species include king and silver salmon, char, grayling, and rainbow trout.

Rainbow King Lodge
Ray Loesche
Box 106
Iliamna AK 99606

Fully modern lodge with private baths conducts seven-day-only packages with daily fly-outs to trophy fish areas. Located in the Bristol Bay area southwest of Anchorage.

Red Quill Lodge
Larry Bryant
Box 49
Iliamna AK 99606

Hunting and fishing lodge on Lake Iliamna with daily fly-outs to fishing locations. Serves a limited number of guests. Lodge maintains remote tent camps for sport hunting.

Royal Coachman Lodge
Bill Martin
Box 10068
Dillingham AK 99576

Lodge located sixty-five miles north of Dillingham on the Nuyakuk River at the outlet of Tikchik Lakes. Guest rooms, lounge, bar and dining room. Winter address: Box 1887, Anchorage AK 99510.

Samsal's Rainbow River Lodge
Fishing International
4000 Montgomery Drive
Santa Rosa CA 95405

This lodge is world famous for trophy rainbows. Located on the Copper River in the Iliamna trophy fishing area. Rates include lodging, meals, fly-out jetboat fishing, and round trip from Iliamna.

Talarik Creek Lodge
Floyd Polmateer
Box 68
Iliamna AK 99606

Year-round lodge with accommodations for twenty-seven in the Iliamna-Mulchatna area. Modern lodge with family-style meals. Guided fly-out sportfishing for rainbow, char, grayling, and salmon.

Tikchik Narrows Lodge
Bob Curtis
Box 1631
Anchorage AK 99510

Located sixty-five miles northwest of Dillingham, this full-facility lodge offers carpeted cabins, family-style meals, daily flying side trips, and superb sportfishing.

Valhalla Lodge
Kirk Gay, Alaska Safari, Inc.
Box 6583
Anchorage AK 99502

Private lodge located amid scenic rivers and lakes near beautiful 200-foot waterfall offers clearwater sportfishing for twelve people. Eight species of sportfish in area.

Van Valin's Island Lodge
Glen Van Valin
Port Alsworth AK 99653

Remote fly-in lodge located 150 miles southwest of Anchorage on the scenic upper end of Lake Clark. Log main lodge and cabins, homestyle meals, fly-outs, float trips, camping and photography.

Wood River Lodge
Ken Stockholm
4437 Stanford
Fairbanks AK 99701

Lodge located forty miles north of Dillingham in the Wood-Tikchik area on the Agulowak River. Trout and grayling fifty feet from lodge; daily fly-outs for salmon. Boats, motors, and experienced guides.

Appendix A:
Populations (1980) and Zip Codes

Town	Population	Zip Code
Akhiok	103	99615
Akiachak	378	99551
Akiak	229	99552
Akolmiut	353	N/A
Akutan	188	99553
Alakanuk	546	99554
Aleknagik	232	99555
Allakaket	169	99720
Ambler	202	99786
Anaktuvuk Pass	250	99721
Anchorage	243,829	995--
Eastchester Station		99501
Main Office		99502
Contract Station #1		99503
Contract Station #3		99504
Fort Richardson		99505
Elmendorf AFB		99506
Contract Station #4		99507
Mountain View Station		99508
Spenard Station		99509
Downtown Station		99510
South Station		99511
Alyeska Pipeline Co.		99512
Federal Building		99513
Anchor Point	317	99556
Anderson	522	99790
Angoon	562	99820
Aniak	351	99557
Annette	139	99926
Anvik	115	99558
Arctic Village	111	99722
Atka	93	99502
Atmautluak	236	99559

Town	Population	Zip Code
Auke Bay	N/A	99821
Barrow	2,943	99723
Beaver	66	99724
Belkofski	N/A	99695
Bethel	3,683	99559
Bettles Field	N/A	99726
Big Lake	410	99687
Border	N/A	99780
Brevig Mission	134	99785
Buckland	217	99727
Cantwell	89	99729
Cape Yakataga	N/A	99574
Central	36	99730
Chalkyitsik	100	99788
Chatanika	N/A	99701
Chefornak	244	99561
Chevak	513	99563
Chicken	37	99732
Chignik	178	99564
Chignik Lagoon	48	99565
Chignik Lake	138	99564
Chitina	42	99566
Chuathbaluk	124	99557
Chugiak	N/A	99567
Circle	101	99733
Clam Gulch	50	99568
Clarks Point	80	99569
Clear	N/A	99704
Cold Bay	250	99571
Cooper Landing	116	99572
Copper Center	213	99573
Cordova	2,244	99574
Craig	604	99921
Crooked Creek	108	99575
Curry's Corner	N/A	99710
Deadhorse	64	99734
Deering	158	99736
Delta Junction	1,163	99737
Denali Park	32	99755
Dillingham	1,791	99576
Diomede	134	N/A
Dot Lake	67	99737
Douglas	N/A	99824
Dutch Harbor	N/A	99692
Eagle	142	99738
Eagle River	N/A	99577
Eek	235	99578
Egegik	75	99579
Ekwok	78	99580

Town	Population	Zip Code
Elfin Cove	28	99825
Elim	205	99739
Emmonak	581	99581
Ester	149	99725
Fairbanks	27,103	997--
Borough Population, 1984	64,186	
Main Office		99701
Eielson AFB		99702
Fort Wainwright		99703
Main Office Boxes		99706
Downtown Station		99707
College Branch		99708
Salcha		99714
False Pass	70	99583
Flat	N/A	99684
Fortuna Ledge	260	99585
Fort Yukon	625	99740
Gakona	87	99586
Galena	847	99741
Gambell	432	99742
Girdwood	N/A	99587
Glennallen	511	99588
Golovin	112	99762
Goodnews Bay	173	99589
Grayling	211	99590
Gustavus	98	99826
Haines	1,078	99827
Healy	334	99743
Holy Cross	243	99602
Homer	3,237	99603
Hoonah	864	99829
Hooper Bay	651	99604
Hope	103	99605
Houston	826	99694
Hughes	74	99745
Huslia	241	99746
Hydaburg	412	99922
Hyder	77	99923
Iliamna	94	99606
Juneau	23,729	998--
Main Office		99801
Main Office Boxes		99802
Mendenhall Station		99803
State Government Offices		99811
Kachemak	288	N/A
Kake	631	99830
Kakovik	214	99747
Kalskag	N/A	99607
Kaltag	246	99748

Appendix A

Town	Population	Zip Code
Karluk	96	99608
Kasaan	70	N/A
Kasigluk	328	99609
Kasilof	201	99610
Kenai	5,721	99611
Ketchikan	7,778	99901
Kiana	364	99749
King Cove	523	99612
King Salmon	545	99613
Kipnuk	371	99614
Kivalina	253	99750
Klawock	433	99925
Kobuk	64	99751
Kodiak	5,873	99615
Koghanok	83	99606
Koliganek	117	99576
Kongiganak	239	99559
Kotlik	347	99620
Kotzebue	2,470	99752
Koyuk	183	99753
Koyukuk	99	99754
Kupreanof	54	N/A
Kwethluk	467	99621
Kwigillingok	354	99622
Lake Minchumina	N/A	99757
Larsen Bay	180	99624
Levelock	79	99625
Lower Kalskag	260	99626
Manley Hot Springs	61	99756
Manokotak	299	99628
McGrath	498	99627
Medfra	N/A	99629
Mekoryuk	178	99630
Metlakatla	1,056	99926
Meyers Chuck	50	99903
Minto	153	99758
Moose Pass	76	99631
Mountain Village	601	99632
Naknek	318	99633
Napakiak	286	99634
Napaskiak	251	99559
Nenana	475	99760
Newhalen	140	N/A
New Stuyahok	337	99636
Newtok	175	99681
Nightmute	141	99690
Nikishka	1,109	99611
Nikolai	110	99691
Nikolski	50	99638

Town	Population	Zip Code
Ninilchik	341	99639
Noatak	273	99761
Nome	3,430	99762
Nondalton	176	99640
Noorvik	518	99763
North Pole	942	99705
Northway	73	99764
Nuiqsut	287	99723
Nulato	353	99765
Nunapitchuk	N/A	99641
Nyac	N/A	99642
Old Harbor	355	99643
Ouzinkie	233	99644
Palmer	2,542	99645
Paxson	30	99737
Pedro Bay	33	99647
Pelican	185	99832
Perryville	111	99648
Petersburg	3,040	99833
Pilot Point	66	99649
Pilot Station	337	99650
Pitkas Point	88	99658
Platinum	57	99651
Point Baker	90	99927
Point Hope	544	99766
Port Alexander	98	99836
Port Alsworth	N/A	99653
Port Graham	161	99603
Port Heiden	94	99549
Port Lions	291	99550
Quinhagak	427	99655
Rampart	50	99767
Red Devil	39	99656
Ruby	214	99768
Russian Mission	175	99657
Saint George	158	99660
Saint Marys	442	99658
Saint Michael	295	99659
Saint Paul	595	99660
Sand Point	797	99661
Savoonga	477	99769
Saxman	273	N/A
Scammon Bay	251	99662
Selawik	602	99770
Seldovia	733	99663
Seward	1,839	99664
Shageluk	132	99665
Shaktoolik	159	99771
Sheldon Point	107	99666

Town	Population	Zip Code
Shishmaref	425	99772
Shungnak	214	99773
Sitka	8,223	99835
Skagway	790	98840
Skwentna	N/A	99667
Slana	49	99586
Sleetmute	107	99668
Soldotna	3,353	99669
South Naknek	145	99670
Stebbins	321	99671
Sterling	919	99672
Stevens Village	96	99774
Stony River	62	99557
Sutton	182	99674
Takotna	48	99675
Talkeetna	441	99676
Tanacross	117	99776
Tanana	486	99777
Tatitlek	68	99677
Teller	206	99778
Tenakee Springs	141	99841
Tetlin	107	99779
Thorne Bay	316	N/A
Togiak	507	99678
Tok	589	99780
Toksook Bay	357	99637
Trapper Creek	N/A	99688
Tuluksak	243	99679
Tuntutuliak	216	99680
Tununak	302	99681
Twin Hills	70	99576
Tyonek	239	99682
Unalakleet	604	99684
Unalaska	1,922	99685
Upper Kalskag	133	N/A
Usibelli	53	99787
Valdez	3,698	99686
Venetie	132	99781
Wainwright	436	99782
Wales	129	99783
Ward Cove	N/A	99928
Wasilla	3,459	99687
White Mountain	121	99784
Whittier	224	99693
Willow	139	99688
Wrangell	2,376	99929
Yakutat	462	99689

Appendix B:
Times and Temperatures

Alaska's Time Zones

On October 30th, 1983, a plan to reduce the number of time zones in Alaska from four to two went into effect. Nearly all of Alaska, including Southeast, was placed on Yukon time, which is only one hour behind Pacific time. The far western portions of the Aleutian Islands and St. Lawrence Island are the only parts of Alaska still on Alaska standard time.

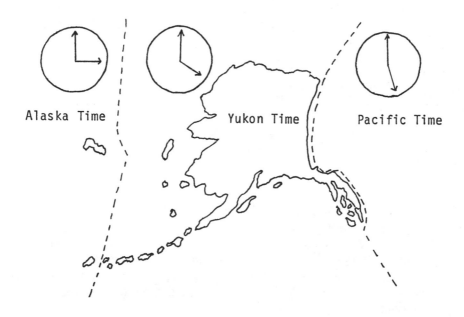

Alaska Time   Yukon Time   Pacific Time

Summer Maximum Daylight Hours

	Anchorage	Barrow	Fairbanks	Juneau	Ketchikan
Sunrise	4:21 a.m.	May 10	12:59 a.m.	3:51 a.m.	4:04 a.m.
Sunset	11:42 p.m.	Aug 2	10:48 p.m.	10:09 p.m.	9:33 p.m.
Hours of Daylight	19 hrs. 21 min.	84 days	21 hrs. 49 min.	18 hrs. 18 min.	17 hrs. 29 min.
Hours of Darkness	4 hrs. 39 min.	none	2 hrs. 11 min.	5 hrs. 42 min.	6 hrs. 31 min.

Winter Minimum Daylight Hours

	Anchorage	Barrow	Fairbanks	Juneau	Ketchikan
Sunrise	9:14 a.m.	Jan 24	9:59 a.m.	9:46 a.m.	9:12 a.m.
Sunset	2:42 p.m.	Nov 18	1:41 p.m.	4:07 p.m.	4:18 p.m.
Hours of Daylight	5 hrs. 28 min.	none	3 hrs. 42 min.	6 hrs. 21 min.	7 hrs. 6 min.
Hours of Darkness	18 hrs. 32 min.	67 days	20 hrs. 18 min.	17 hrs. 39 min.	16 hrs. 54 min.

Wind Chill Temperatures

Wind chill temperatures are important in Alaska during winter. Not only can wind lower the effective temperature many degrees, but activities such as riding a bike or snowmachine can have the same effect. There is little danger at wind chill temperatures above −20 degrees, but at wind chill temperatures from −20 to −70 degrees, skin can freeze in one minute. There is extreme danger at wind chill factors colder than −70 degrees.

Temperature (Fahrenheit)	Wind Chill Temperatures with Wind Speeds of:			
	10 m.p.h.	*20 m.p.h.*	*30 m.p.h.*	*40 m.p.h.*
40	30	20	10	10
30	15	5	0	− 5
20	5	− 10	− 20	− 20
10	− 10	− 25	− 30	− 35
0	− 20	− 35	− 50	− 55
− 10	− 35	− 50	− 65	− 70
− 20	− 45	− 65	− 80	− 85
− 30	− 60	− 80	− 95	− 100
− 40	− 70	− 95	− 110	− 115
− 50	− 80	− 110	− 125	− 130

Winds above 40 m.p.h. have little additional effect.

[And see chart next page]

Average Monthly Temperatures, Yearly Snowfall, and Average Annual Precipitation

	Jan	Feb	Mar	Apr	May	June	July	Aug	Sept	Oct	Nov	Dec	Yearly Snowfall (inches)	Annual Precipitation (inches)
Anchorage	13	18	24	35	46	54	58	56	48	35	22	14	70	15
Barrow	-24	-14	-16	-2	19	33	44	38	31	14	-1	-13	10	5
Bethel	5	7	11	24	40	51	55	53	45	30	18	3	18	16
Delta Junction	-7	-4	9	27	47	54	59	55	43	19	1	-8	50	11
Fairbanks	-12	-7	9	29	48	60	62	56	45	25	3	-10	69	11
Homer	21	23	27	35	42	49	53	52	47	37	28	22	72	25
Juneau	23	24	31	39	47	53	56	54	49	42	32	27	94	54
Ketchikan	33	35	38	43	49	54	58	59	54	47	40	36	33	154
King Salmon	13	15	20	31	42	50	55	54	47	33	22	12	15	20
Kodiak	31	32	32	37	43	50	54	55	50	41	35	29	84	60
McGrath	-9	-5	9	27	44	55	58	54	44	25	5	-9	52	15
Nome	6	6	7	18	35	45	50	50	42	28	16	4	24	14
Petersburg	26	27	34	40	47	51	56	55	50	43	35	30	103	106
Valdez	22	24	28	37	44	51	54	53	47	38	28	20	250	59

Appendix C:
Cost of Living

Sample Prices

Below are sample prices from four Alaskan cities. Generally, the cost of living in Alaska is fifteen percent to forty percent higher than in the lower forty-eight.

	Anchorage	Fairbanks	Juneau	Nome
Milk, per gallon	$ 3.24	$ 3.40	$ 3.48	$ 5.59
Eggs, per dozen	$ .98	$ 1.05	$ .94	$ 1.59
Lettuce, per lb.	$ .87	$ .82	$ .69	$ 1.79
Loaf of bread	$ .91	$ .85	$ 1.49	$ 2.19
Ground beef, per lb.	$ 1.89	$ 1.63	$ 1.84	$ 1.95
Steak dinner	$ 13.25	$ 14.75	$ 16.50	$ 15.00
Coffee, per cup	$ .70	$ .40	$ .75	$ .50
Ham and eggs	$ 5.08	$ 4.00	$ 4.13	$ 6.38
Hamburger	$ 3.35	$ 4.00	$ 5.18	$ 5.00
Gasoline, per gallon	$ 1.45	$ 1.56	$ 1.34	$ 1.78
Diesel, per gallon	$ 1.26	$ 1.42	$ 1.31	$ 1.39
Car insurance, per yr.	$600.00	$605.00	$325.00	$600.00
Auto tune up	$ 90.00	$ 82.50	$ 52.00	$ 75.00
Heating oil, per gal.	$ 1.05	$ 1.25	$ 1.47	$ 1.73

Housing Costs

	Anchorage	Fairbanks	Juneau	Nome
4-bedroom home (purchase)	$120,000 to $210,000	$115,000 to $135,000	$95,000 to $155,000	$98,000 to $160,000

Appendix C

	Anchorage	Fairbanks	Juneau	Nome
3-bedroom home (purchase)	$87,000 to $166,000	$99,000 to $115,000	$89,000 to $133,000	$91,000 to $138,000
2-bedroom home (purchase)	$77,500 to $98,000	$79,000 to $85,000	$59,000 to $84,500	$62,000 to $87,000
apartment rental 3-bedroom	$675 to $950	$725 to $1,025	$700 to $1,200	$750 up
apartment rental 2-bedroom	$550 to $775	$785 to $850	$625 to $875	$650 up
apartment rental 1-bedroom	$475 to $595	$550 to $675	$575 to $650	$500

Appendix D:
Alaskan Chambers of Commerce and Visitor Centers

Alaska Division of Tourism
Pouch E
Juneau AK 99811

Alaska State Chamber
310 Second Street
Juneau AK 99801
(907) 586-2323

Alaska State Infor. Center
Alaska State Troopers
P.O. Box 335
Tok AK 99780

Anchorage Chamber
415 F. Street
Anchorage AK 99501
(907) 272-2401

Anchorage Visitors Bureau
201 E. Third Avenue
Anchorage AK 99501
(907) 276-4118

Arctic Circle Chamber
Box 284
Kotzebue AK 99752
(907) 442-3401

Chugiak-Eagle River Chamber
Box 249
Eagle River AK 99599

Copper Valley Chamber
Box 113
Copper Center AK 99573

Cordova Chamber
Box 99
Cordova AK 99574
(907) 424-7260

Delta Junction Chamber
Box 978
Delta Junction AK 99737
(907) 895-4439

Dillingham Chamber
Box 236
Dillingham AK 99576

Dillingham (City of)
Box 191
Dillingham AK 99576

Fairbanks Chamber
Box 7446
Fairbanks AK 99701
(907) 452-1105

Fairbanks Visitors Bureau
550 First Avenue
Fairbanks AK 99701
(907) 456-5774

Haines Chamber
Box 518
Haines AK 99827
(907) 766-2202

Homer Chamber
Box 541
Homer AK 99603
(907) 235-7740

Homer Visitors Bureau
Box 2706
Homer AK 99603
(907) 235-7875

Juneau Chamber
1711 Glacier Ave., Suite 207
Juneau AK 99801
(907) 586-6420

Juneau Division of Tourism
Ninth Floor
State Office Building
Juneau AK 99811

Juneau Visitors Bureau
101 Egan Drive
Juneau AK 99801
(907) 586-7989

Kenai Chamber
Box 497
Kenai AK 99611

Kenai Peninsula Visitors Bureau
Box 497
Kenai AK 99611

Ketchikan Chamber
Box 5957
Ketchikan AK 99901

Ketchikan Visitors Bureau
Box 7055
Ketchikan AK 99901
(907) 225-6166

Kodiak Chamber
Box 1485
Kodiak AK 99615
(907) 486-5557

Mid Valley Chamber
Box 193
Houston AK 99694
(907) 892-6540

Mountain View Chamber
4231 Mountain View Drive
Mountain View AK 99504

Nenana Chamber
Box 268
Nenana AK 99760

Nome Visitors Bureau
Box 251
Nome AK 99762
(907) 443-5535

North Pole Chamber
Box 5071
North Pole AK 99705

Palmer Chamber
Box 45
Palmer AK 99645
(907) 745-2880

Petersburg Chamber
Box 529
Petersburg AK 99833
(907) 772-3646

Point Barrow Chamber
Point Barrow AK 99723

Prince of Wales Chamber
Box 227
Craig AK 99921
(907) 828-3377

Seldovia Chamber
Drawer F
Seldovia AK 99663

Seward Chamber
Box 756
Seward AK 99664
(907) 224-3046

Sitka Chamber
Box 638
Sitka AK 99835
(907) 747-8604

Sitka Visitors Bureau
Box 1226
Sitka AK 99835
(907) 747-5940

Skagway Chamber
Box 194
Skagway AK 99840
(907) 983-2264

Skagway Visitors Bureau
Box 415
Skagway AK 99840

Soldotna Chamber
Box 236
Soldotna AK 99669
(907) 262-9814

Talkeetna Chamber
Box 334
Talkeetna AK 99676
(907) 733-2512

Tok Chamber
Box 389
Tok AK 99780
(907) 883-4221

Valdez Chamber
Box 512
Valdez AK 99686
(907) 835-2330

Wasilla Chamber
Box 1300
Wasilla AK 99687
(907) 376-2121

Whittier Chamber
Box 703
Whittier AK 99693
(907) 472-2352

Wrangell Chamber
Box 49
Wrangell AK 99929

Appendix E:
Education

Colleges and Universities

The University of Alaska maintains three senior colleges within the state. The main campus is located in Fairbanks and is the only campus that maintains dormitory facilities. The two other campuses of the University of Alaska are in Anchorage and Juneau.

There are ten community colleges in the university system that are degree-granting institutions. These colleges are located in Anchorage, Bethel, Fairbanks, Ketchikan, Kodiak, Nome, Palmer, Sitka, Soldotna, and Valdez.

Eleven rural education and extension centers are maintained by the university. These are located in Adak, Cold Bay, Delta Junction, Dillingham, Fort Yukon, Galena, McGrath, Nenana, Sand Point, Tok, and Unalaska. These centers offer courses for college credit as well as community service courses.

There are two private institutions of higher learning in the state, one in Anchorage and one in Sitka.

The following is a list of places to write for information on colleges and universities within Alaska.

Senior Colleges

Alaska Pacific University
University Boulevard
Anchorage AK 99504

University of Alaska at Anchorage
2651 Providence Drive
Anchorage AK 99504

Sheldon Jackson College
Box 479
Sitka AK 99835

University of Alaska at Fairbanks
Fairbanks AK 99701

University of Alaska at Juneau
11120 Glacier Highway
Juneau AK 99802

Community Colleges

Anchorage Community College
Providence Drive
Anchorage AK 99504

Kenai Peninsula Community College
Box 848
Soldotna AK 99669

Ketchikan Community College
Box 358
Ketchikan AK 99901

Kodiak Community College
Box 946
Kodiak AK 99615

Kuskokwim Community College
Box 368
Bethel AK 99559

Mat-Su Community College
Box 899
Palmer AK 99645

Northwest Community College
Box 400
Nome AK 99762

Prince William Sound Community
    College
Box 590
Valdez AK 99686

Sheldon Jackson College
Box 479
Sitka AK 99835

Sitka Community College
Box 1090
Sitka AK 99835

Tanana Valley Community
    College, Constitution Hall
University of Alaska
Fairbanks AK 99701

For information on rural education centers write:

University of Alaska Community Colleges
Rural Educational and Extension Affairs
2221 East Northern Lights Boulevard
Anchorage AK 99504

School Districts

There are fifty-three public school districts in the state of Alaska. Thirty-two of these are located in cities; the other twenty-one are outside of any organized city or borough.

Adak Region Schools
Adak Naval Station
Box 34
FPO Seattle WA 98791

Alaska Gateway Schools
Box 226
Tok AK 99780

Aleutian Region School District
Technical Center
640 West 36th Ave.
Anchorage AK 99503

Anchorage Schools
4600 DeBarr Road
Pouch 6-614
Anchorage AK 99502

Annette Island Schools
Box 7
Metlakatla AK 99926

Bering Strait Schools
Box 225
Unalakeet AK 99684

Bristol Bay Borough Schools
Box 169
Naknek AK 99633

Chatham Schools
Box 109
Angoon AK 99820

Chugach Schools
Box 638
Whittier AK 99639

Copper River Schools
Box 103
Glennallen AK 99588

Cordova City Schools
Box 140
Cordova AK 99574

Craig City Schools
Box 71
Craig AK 99921

Delta/Greely Schools
Box 527
Delta Junction AK 99737

Dillingham City Schools
Box 202
Dillingham AK 99576

Fairbanks North Star
Borough Schools
Box 1250
Fairbanks AK 99701

Galena City Schools
Box 299
Galena AK 99741

Haines Borough Schools
Box 636
Haines AK 99827

Hoonah City Schools
Box 157
Hoonah AK 99829

Hydaburg City Schools
Box 109
Hydaburg AK 99922

Iditarod Area Schools
Box 105
McGrath AK 99627

Juneau Borough Schools
Box 808
Douglas AK 99824

Kake City Schools
Box 450
Kake AK 99830

Kenai Peninsula
Borough Schools
Box 1200
Soldotna AK 99669

Ketchikan Gateway
Borough Schools
Pouch Z
Ketchikan AK 99901

King Cove City Schools
Box 6
King Cove AK 99612

Klawock City Schools
Box 9
Klawock AK 99925

Kodiak Island Borough Schools
Box 886
Kodiak AK 99615

Kuspuk Schools
Box 108
Aniak AK 99557

Lake & Peninsula Schools
Box 498
King Salmon AK 99613

Lower Kuskokwim Schools
Box 305
Bethel AK 99559

Lower Yukon Schools
Box 200
Mountain Village AK 99632

Mat-Su Borough Schools
Box AB
Palmer AK 99645

Nenana City Schools
Box 10
Nenana AK 99760

Nome City Schools
Box 131
Nome AK 99762

North Slope Borough Schools
Box 169
Barrow AK 99723

Northwest Arctic Schools
Box 51
Kotzebue AK 99752

Pelican City Schools
Box 603
Pelican AK 99832

Petersburg City Schools
Box 289
Petersburg AK 99833

Pribilof Schools
Saint Paul Island AK 99660

Railbelt School District
Drawer 129
Healy AK 99743

St. Marys Public Schools
Box 71
Saint Marys AK 99658

Sand Point School District
Box 158
Sand Point AK 99661

Sitka Borough Schools
Box 179
Sitka AK 99835

Skagway City Schools
Box 497
Skagway AK 99840

Southeast Island Schools
Box 8340
Ketchikan AK 99901

Southwest Region Schools
Box 196
Dillingham AK 99576

Tanana City Schools
Box 89
Tanana AK 99777

Unalaska City Schools
Pouch 260
Unalaska AK 99685

Valdez City Schools
Box 398
Valdez AK 99686

Wrangell City Schools
Box 651
Wrangell AK 99929

Yakutat City Schools
Box 427
Yakutat AK 99689

Yukon Flat Schools
Box 359
Fort Yukon AK 99740

Yukon/Koyukuk Schools
Box 309
Nenana AK 99760

Appendix F:
Other Information Sources

Agriculture

Cooperative Extension Service
University of Alaska
Fairbanks AK 99701

State Division of Agriculture
Pouch A
Wasilla AK 99687

Business

Alaska Dept. of Commerce
and Economic Development
Pouch D
Juneau AK 99801

Census Data
Alaska Dept. of Labor
Administrative Services Division
P.O. Box 1149
Juneau AK 99811

Department of Health
and Social Services
Pouch H-01
Juneau AK 99811

State Chamber of Commerce
310 Second Street
Juneau AK 99801

State Department of Labor
Box 1149
Juneau AK 99811

State Employment Service
Box 3-7000
Juneau AK 99802

Housing

Cook Inlet Housing Authority
670 West Fireweed Lane
Anchorage AK 99503

State Housing Authority
P.O. Box 80
Anchorage AK 99510

209

Maps

Distribution Section
U.S. Geological Survey
Federal Center
Denver CO 80225

Distribution Section
U.S. Geological Survey
1200 So. Eads Street
Arlington VA 22202

National Forests

U.S. Department of Interior
National Park Service
540 West 5th Avenue
Anchorage AK 99501

USDA Forest Service
Tongass National Forest
P.O. Box 1628
Juneau AK 99802

USDA Forest Service
Chugach National Forest
121 Fireweed Lane
Anchorage AK 99501

National Parks

Aniakchak National Monument
Box 7
King Salmon AK 99613

Kenai Fjords National Park
P.O. Box 1727
Seward AK 99664

Bering Land Bridge Nat. Monument
P.O. Box 220
Nome AK 99762

Klondike Goldrush Nat. Park
P.O. Box 517
Skagway AK 99840

Cape Krusenstern Nat. Monument
P.O. Box 287
Kotzebue AK 99752

Kobuk Valley National Park
P.O. Box 287
Kotzebue AK 99752

Denali Nat. Park and Preserve
National Park Service
McKinley Park AK 99755

Lake Clark Nat. Park & Preserve
P.O. Box 61
Anchorage AK 99513

Gates of the Arctic Nat. Park
P.O. Box 74680
Fairbanks AK 99707

Noatak National Preserve
P.O. Box 287
Kotzebue AK 99752

Glacier Bay National Park
P.O. Box 1089
Juneau AK 99806

Wrangell–St. Elias National Park
P.O. Box 29
Glennallen AK 99588

Katmai National Park & Preserve
P.O. Box 7
King Salmon AK 99613

Yukon-Charley Rivers Nat. Preserve
P.O. Box 64
Eagle AK 99738

Resources

Alaska Miners Association
509 W. Third Ave., Suite 17
Anchorage AK 99501

Alaska Oil and Gas Association
505 W. Northern Lights Blvd.
Anchorage AK 99503

Mines Information Office
3327 Fairbanks Street
Anchorage AK 99503

State Division of Surveys
3001 Porcupine Drive
Anchorage AK 99501

Index

A

B

213

M

N